D1576643

C016676672

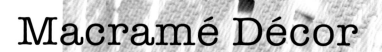

# Macramé Décor

## 25 Boho-Chic Patterns and Project Ideas

**Märchen Art Studio**

# Preface

In recent years, "boho-chic style" interior decoration has been trending. "Boho" is a neologism that combines bohemian and SoHo—the area in New York. It has been said that "boho-chic" originated from the style of fashionable SoHo women as they began to incorporate bohemian styles into their overall fashion sense. Their unconventional style caught the world's attention. "Boho-chic" has influenced interior design trends and created an eccentric interior decoration style. For example, it freely incorporates colorful traditional patterned fabrics with modern furniture pieces. It is artistic, but relaxing and comfortable at the same time. It's safe to say that this is the true charm of boho style interior decoration.

Major décor items employed in such boho style interior decoration are created with macramé, which is of course known for its use in plant hangers and tapestries. Macramé is a handcraft that creates items in a simple manner—you just "manually make knots with cords." The types of knots and their combinations are virtually unlimited. Cords, planes, solid bodies, etc. Macramé is capable of creating a huge variety of objects, shapes, and patterns.

Simply adding a single macramé item to your space will dramatically change the overall feel of the space. If the macramé item is handmade, you can determine its size and design while having fun making the item. Shall we begin making macramé items and decorating your space in boho style?

# CONTENTS

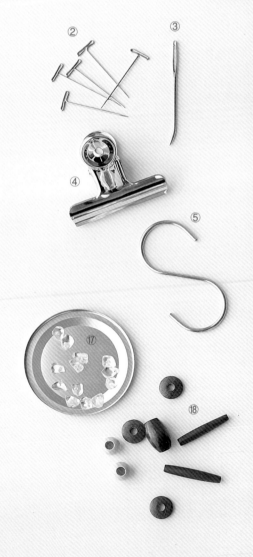

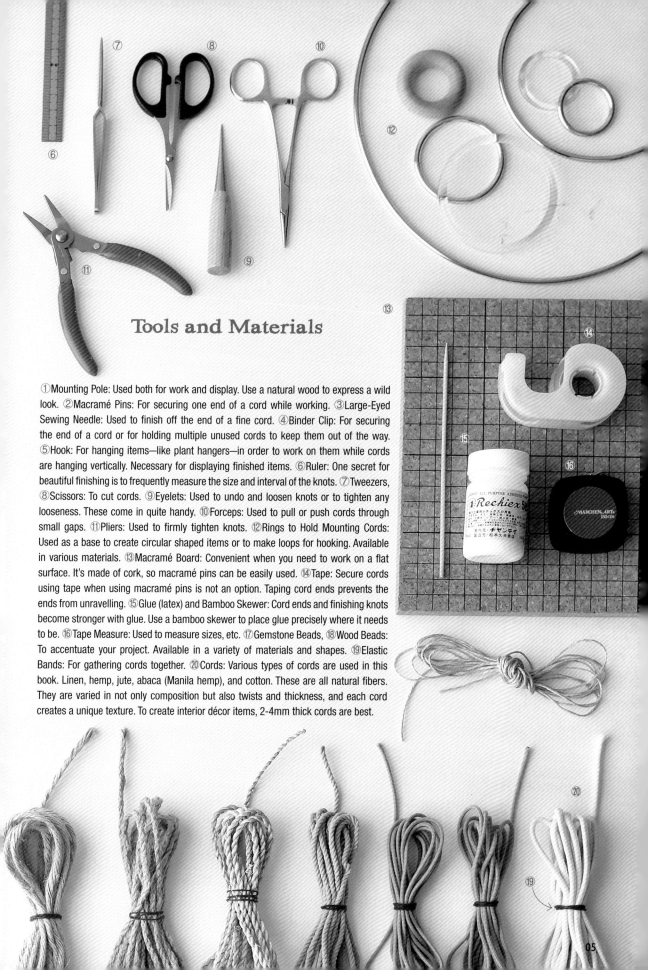

# Tools and Materials

①Mounting Pole: Used both for work and display. Use a natural wood to express a wild look. ②Macramé Pins: For securing one end of a cord while working. ③Large-Eyed Sewing Needle: Used to finish off the end of a fine cord. ④Binder Clip: For securing the end of a cord or for holding multiple unused cords to keep them out of the way. ⑤Hook: For hanging items—like plant hangers—in order to work on them while cords are hanging vertically. Necessary for displaying finished items. ⑥Ruler: One secret for beautiful finishing is to frequently measure the size and interval of the knots. ⑦Tweezers, ⑧Scissors: To cut cords. ⑨Eyelets: Used to undo and loosen knots or to tighten any looseness. These come in quite handy. ⑩Forceps: Used to pull or push cords through small gaps. ⑪Pliers: Used to firmly tighten knots. ⑫Rings to Hold Mounting Cords: Used as a base to create circular shaped items or to make loops for hooking. Available in various materials. ⑬Macramé Board: Convenient when you need to work on a flat surface. It's made of cork, so macramé pins can be easily used. ⑭Tape: Secure cords using tape when using macramé pins is not an option. Taping cord ends prevents the ends from unravelling. ⑮Glue (latex) and Bamboo Skewer: Cord ends and finishing knots become stronger with glue. Use a bamboo skewer to place glue precisely where it needs to be. ⑯Tape Measure: Used to measure sizes, etc. ⑰Gemstone Beads, ⑱Wood Beads: To accentuate your project. Available in a variety of materials and shapes. ⑲Elastic Bands: For gathering cords together. ⑳Cords: Various types of cords are used in this book. Linen, hemp, jute, abaca (Manila hemp), and cotton. These are all natural fibers. They are varied in not only composition but also twists and thickness, and each cord creates a unique texture. To create interior décor items, 2-4mm thick cords are best.

# Knot Variations

This page shows a variety of the knots used in this book.
Each knot looks like it is squirming, as if it were a little creature.
Please refer to the page indicated for each knot's tying method.

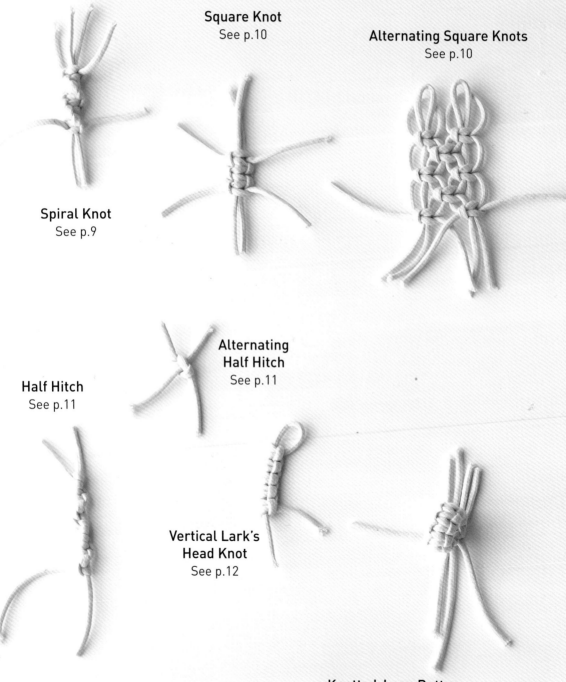

**Square Knot**
See p.10

**Alternating Square Knots**
See p.10

**Spiral Knot**
See p.9

**Alternating Half Hitch**
See p.11

**Half Hitch**
See p.11

**Vertical Lark's Head Knot**
See p.12

**Knotted-Loop Button**
See p.12

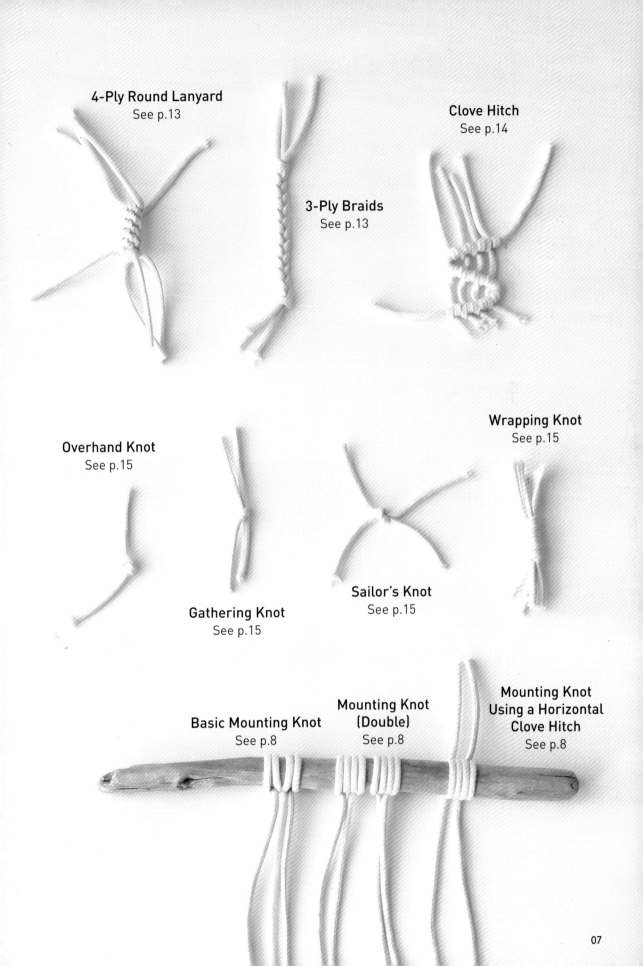

**4-Ply Round Lanyard**
See p.13

**3-Ply Braids**
See p.13

**Clove Hitch**
See p.14

**Wrapping Knot**
See p.15

**Overhand Knot**
See p.15

**Gathering Knot**
See p.15

**Sailor's Knot**
See p.15

**Basic Mounting Knot**
See p.8

**Mounting Knot (Double)**
See p.8

**Mounting Knot Using a Horizontal Clove Hitch**
See p.8

# Macramé Basic Techniques

**Mounting Knots** These are the methods for mounting working cords that most macramé projects require in the beginning. Mounting knots can be tied to a bar or a ring, depending on your project.

## Basic Mounting Knot

This is the basic knot most used when attaching a working cord to an anchor cord. The working cord is usually folded in half. In some cases, the working cord is folded unevenly on purpose.

Knot Symbol >>

**1**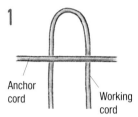
Anchor cord / Working cord
Fold a working cord in half and place it under the anchor cord.

**2**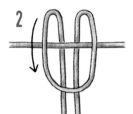
Fold down the loop of the working cord over the anchor cord.

**3**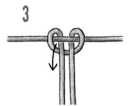
Pull the working ends through the loop, then pull them firmly to tighten the knot.

## Basic Mounting Knot (Reverse)

This is also a basic mounting knot but the position of the loop of the working cord is inverted. The head of the knot faces forward.

Knot Symbol >>

**1**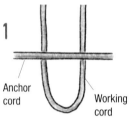
Anchor cord / Working cord
Fold a working cord in half and place it under the anchor cord. The loop of the working cord is facing downward.

**2**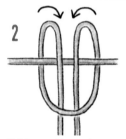
Pull the working ends through the loop.

**3**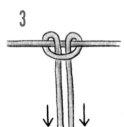
Pull the working ends firmly to tighten the knot.

## Mounting Knot (Double)

After making one Basic Mounting Knot, make another one on each side. Use this when you intend to make a wide knot.

Knot Symbol >>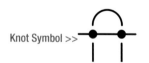

**1**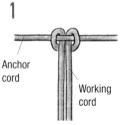
Anchor cord / Working cord
Tie one working cord to the anchor cord in the same manner as the Basic Mounting Knot.

**2**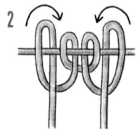
Move the working end over and then under the anchor cord on each side.

**3**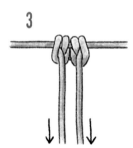
Pull the working end firmly to tighten the knot.

## Using a Horizontal Clove Hitch

This is the method for attaching a working cord using a Horizontal Clove Hitch.

Knot Symbol >>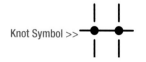

**1**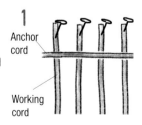
Anchor cord / Working cord
Pin working cords and then lay the anchor cord over the working cords.

**2**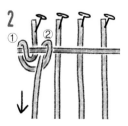
Move the working end over then under the anchor cord on the left, then do the same on the right. Then, pull the working end firmly to tighten the knot.

**3**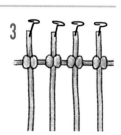
Repeat step 2 the same number of times as there are working cords in your project.

This section introduces eleven different knots used to create the items presented in this book. Unless an instruction specifies "left-facing" or "right-facing" you can choose whichever you prefer. However, the heads of the knots should all be facing the same direction within your project.

## Left-Twisted Spiral Knot

Make a figure-four with two working cords to tie a knot. To repeat, the knot twists downward to the right.

Knot Symbol >>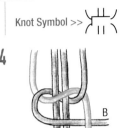

**1**

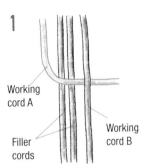

Working cord A

Filler cords

Working cord B

Move working cord A over the filler cords, then move working cord B over working cord A (the working cords make a figure-four).

**2**

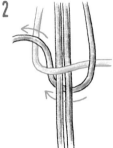

Move working cord B under the filler cords and over working cord A.

**3**

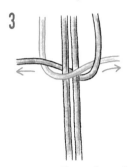

Pull both working cords evenly to the left and right. One spiral knot is tied.

**4**

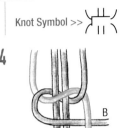

B

A

Move working cord B to the right, passing it over the filler cords. Move working cord A over working cord B.

**5**

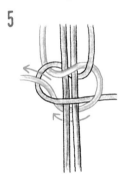

Move working cord A to the left, passing it under the filler cords and through the left loop of working cord B.

**6**

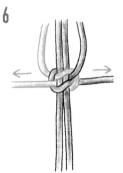

Pull both working cords evenly to left and right. The second Spiral Knot is done.

**7**

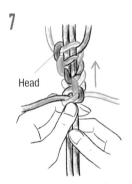

Head

Make five Spiral Knots, then rotate them to the right so the two working cords switch places. Then, push the knots close together to tighten.

### Notes

#### "Knot Symbol" and "Knotting Diagram"

• Instructions for macramé items introduced in this book are described with a "Knot Symbol" (which symbolizes the knot type) and "Knotting Diagram" (which describes rows and length of the sennit).

• The "Knot Symbol" describes a knot while simplifying its features and how it is tied. Please familiarize yourself with the Knot Symbol of each knot.

• "Knotting Diagram" is a blueprint for macramé items. Please refer to the "Macramé Basic Techniques" section if you don't remember which knot type the symbol indicates.

Example: Knotting Diagram for a five row Left-Twisted Spiral Knot

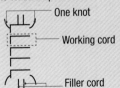

One knot

Working cord

Filler cord

## Right-Twisted Spiral Knot

Reverse the left and right side of your Left-Facing Spiral Knot. It makes a downward left spiral.

Knot Symbol >>

**1**

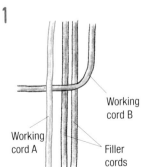

Working cord B

Working cord A

Filler cords

Move working cord B over the filler cords, then move working cord A over working cord B (they make a reversed figure-four).

**2**

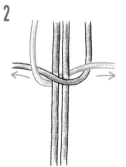

Move working cord A so it passes under the filler cords and over working cord B. Pull both working cords evenly to the left and right.

**3**

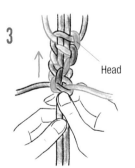

Head

Repeat steps 1 and 2. When the knots cover half of the filler cords, rotate to the right so the two working cords switch places. Then, push the knots close together to tighten.

## Left-Facing Square Knot

Tie a "Left-Twisted Spiral Knot" and a "Right-Twisted Spiral Knot" alternately to make a "Square Knot." Move the leftmost working cord to make a Left-Facing Square Knot.

Knot Symbol >>

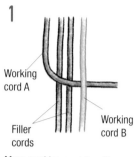

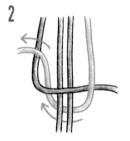

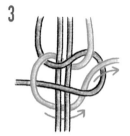

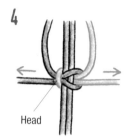

**1** Move working cord A so it passes over the filler cords, then move working cord B over working cord A (they make a figure-four).

**2** Move working cord B passing it under the filler cords and over working cord A. Pull both working cords evenly to left and right (one half knot is tied).

**3** As shown above, reverse the way the working cords are crossed and repeat steps 1 and 2.

**4** Now, one Left-Facing Square Knot is complete. The head of the knot faces left.

## Right-Facing Square Knot

Tie a Right-Facing Square Knot, similar to the "Left-Facing Square Knot" but in reverse. The head of the knot faces on the right side. Regardless of the position of the head, both knots look similar when a sennit is made.

Knot Symbol >>

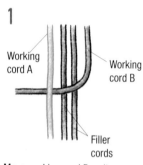

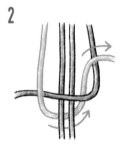

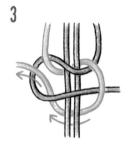

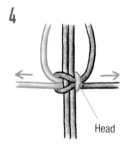

**1** Move working cord B so it passes over the filler cords, then move working cord A over working cord B (they make a reverse figure-four).

**2** Move working cord A so it passes under the filler cords and over working cord B. Pull both working cords evenly to the left and right (one half knot is tied).

**3** As shown above, reverse the way the working cords are crossed and repeat steps 1 and 2.

**4** Now, one Right-Facing Square Knot is complete. The head of the knot faces right.

## Alternating Square Knots

This is a standard technique to create a sennit with a Square Knot. Shifting the position of the Square Knot on every other row creates a plane and interconnected, woven design. Proceed to tie a knot horizontally to make the knots in the same row nice and flat.

**Knotting Diagram**

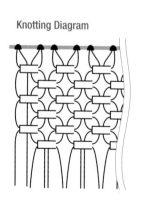

**1** 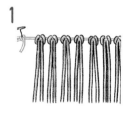 Mount as many cords (must be a multiple of four) as you need.

**2** First → row 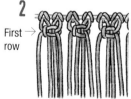 For the first row, tie Square Knots with groups of four cords from left to right.

**3** Second → row 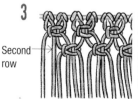 For the second row, shift two cords to the right and begin to tie Square Knots.

**4**  Repeat steps 2 and 3.

## Left-Facing Half Hitch

Wrapping a working cord around the filler cords repeatedly creates a screw-like sennit. A "Left-Facing Half Hitch" creates a right downward spiral.

Knot Symbol >>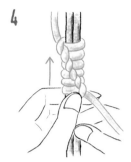

**1**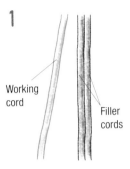

Working cord

Filler cords

Prepare a working cord four to five times longer than its finished size and place it to the left of the filler cords.

**2**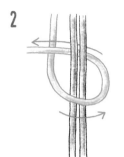

Wrap the working cord around the filler cords counter-clockwise.

**3**

As you pull the working end, pass it over the working cord and tighten the knot. One Left-Facing Half Hitch knot is now complete.

**4**

Repeat steps 2 and 3. Once the spiral of knots is halfway around the filler cords, push the knots together to tighten.

## Right-Facing Half Hitch

Tie a Right-Facing Half Hitch similar to the "Left-Facing Half Hitch," but in reverse. The knots make a downward left spiral. You can use as many filler cords as you need.

Knot Symbol >>

**1**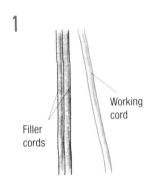

Filler cords

Working cord

Prepare a working cord four to five times longer than its finished size, and place it on the right-side of the filler cords.

**2**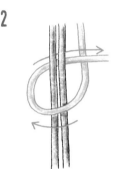

Wrap the working cord around the filler cords in a clockwise direction.

**3**

As you pull the working end, pass it over the working cord and tighten. One Right-Facing Half Hitch knot is now complete.

**4**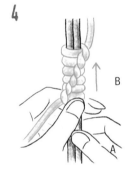

B

A

Repeat steps 2 and 3. Once the spiral knots go halfway around the filler cords, push the knots close together to tighten.

## Alternating Half Hitch

Tie a Right-Facing Half Hitch and a Left-Facing Half Hitch alternately using two cords. Since the working cord and the filler cords switch places in each knot, be careful not to mistake them.

Knot Symbol >>

**1**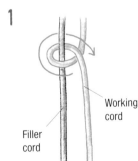

Working cord

Filler cord

Let the cord on the left be the filler cord and the other be the working cord, tie one "Right-Facing Half Hitch (see above)."

**2**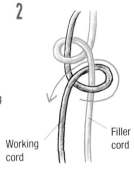

Working cord

Filler cord

Let the cord on the right be the filler cord and the other be the working cord, tie one "Left-Facing Half Hitch (see above).

**3**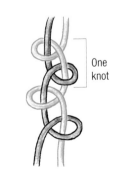

One knot

Now, one Alternating Half Hitch knot is complete. Repeat the above steps to create a sennit.

### Notes

#### The Beginning of an Alternating Half Hitch

Generally speaking, you can start an Alternating Half Hitch with either a "Right-Facing Half Hitch" or a "Left-Facing Half Hitch." However, the Knot Symbol will tell you which knot to begin using first. For example, the above Knot Symbol has a "Right-Facing Half Hitch" on top, so it begins with that knot.

## Left-Facing Vertical Lark's Head

The knot heads are stacked on one side. The head of the "Left-Facing Vertical Lark's Head" is on the left side. The working cord is always on the left side of the filler cord.

Knot Symbol >>

**1**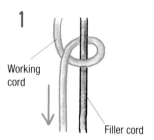

Working cord

Filler cord

Place the working cord on the left of the filler cord. Wrap the working cord around the filler cord counter-clockwise. Pull the working end over the working cord. Then, tighten the knot.

**2**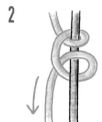

Wrap the working cord around the filler cord counter-clockwise, passing under the filler cord. Pull the working end through the loop of the working cord. Then, tighten the knot.

**3**

Now, one Left-Facing Vertical Lark's Head is complete.

**4**

Repeat steps 1 and 2 to create a sennit.

---

## Right-Facing Vertical Lark's Head

Tie a Right-Facing Vertical Lark's Head by reversing the way the working cord is wrapped around the filler cord. The head of the knot is now on the right side. The working cord is always on the right side of the filler cord.

Knot Symbol >>

**1**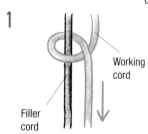

Working cord

Filler cord

Place the working cord to the right of the filler cord. Wrap the working cord around the filler cord clockwise, while passing over the filler cord. Pull the working end over the working cord. Then, tighten.

**2**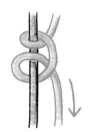

Wrap the working cord around the filler cord clockwise, while passing under the filler cord. Pull the working end through the loop of the working cord. Then, tighten.

**3**

Now, one Right-Facing Vertical Lark's Head Knot is complete.

**4**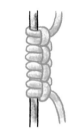

Repeat steps 1 and 2 to create a sennit.

---

## Knotted-Loop Button

This is a technique for forming a button by rolling-up the end of a square knot sennit. The number inside of the Knot Symbol is the number of rows that form the button.

Knot Symbol >>

**1**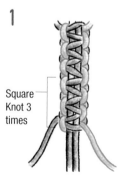

Square Knot 3 times

Make as many Square Knots as the number inside of Knot Symbol (in this case is 3).

**2**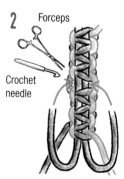

Forceps

Crochet needle

Using a crochet needle or forceps, put the filler cord between the working cord and the filler cord on the third Square Knot from the end of the sennit.

**3**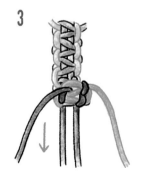

Pull down on the filler cords to roll up the end of the sennit and create a button-like form.

**4**

Tie one Square Knot under the button to secure the end of the sennit. The Knotted-Loop Button is complete.

## 4-Ply Round Lanyard

Four cords are crossed in sequence making a parallel cross pattern. Tying this knot in repetition creates a column-shaped sennit as the head of the knot shifts its position.

Knot Symbol >>

### 1

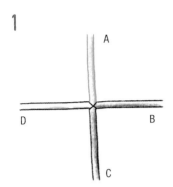

Prepare four cords that are five to six times longer than the finished size and place them in a cross shape (you can use two cords that are ten to twelve times longer than the finished size as well).

### 2

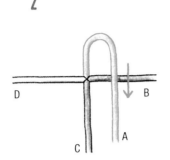

Move cord A, passing it over cord B parallel to cord C.

### 3

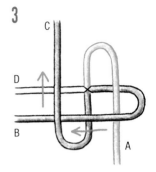

Move cord B, passing over cords A and C. Move cord C, passing over cords B and D.

### 4

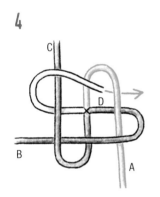
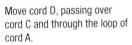

Move cord D, passing over cord C and through the loop of cord A.

### 5

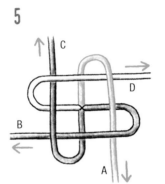

Lightly pull each cord, one at a time, to tighten the knot.

### 6

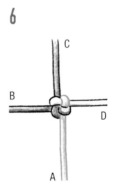

Now one 4-Ply Round Lanyard is complete.

### 7

Repeat steps 2 through 5 to create a sennit.

## 3-Ply Braid

Since a 3-Ply Braid is also a standard method of braiding hair, many people may feel confident with this. Cross three cords, alternately passing over the cord in the middle.

Knot Symbol >>

### 1

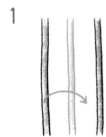

Move cord A by crossing over cord B.

### 2

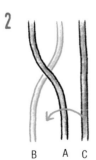

Move cord C while crossing over cord A.

### 3

Move cord B while crossing over cord C.

### 4

Repeat steps 2 and 3. Tighten as you braid the cords.

## Vertical Clove Hitch

Two horizontal knot heads are stacked on top of each other to make one Vertical Clove Hitch Knot. Since the working cord isn't anchored, you can use different colored cords as you knot. This allows you to make your desired pattern.

Knot Symbol >>

**1**

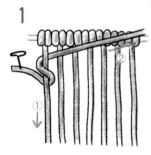

Pin the beginning of the working cord on the left-side. Then, wrap the working cord around the leftmost filler cord, passing under then over the filler cord. Pull the filler cord down firmly (①), then tighten the working cord (②).

**2**

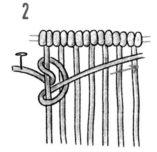

Next, move the working cord while passing over then under the filler cord and through the loop of the working cord. Then, tighten the knot.

**3**

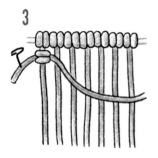

One Vertical Clove Hitch Knot is complete.

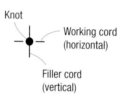

Knot

Working cord (horizontal)

Filler cord (vertical)

**4**

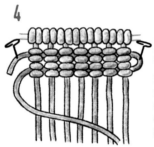

Repeat steps 1 and 2 until you reach the end of the row. Then, move on to the next row. Repeat steps 1 and 2 reversing the way the working cord wrapped around the filler cord and begin tying from the rightmost filler cord to the left.

## Diagonal Clove Hitch

This is the method for tying a diagonal Horizontal Clove Hitch (p.8). This method is often used when creating diamond shapes, etc.

Knot Symbol >>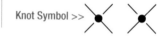

**1**

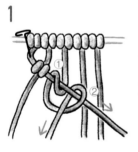

In a similar manner to the Horizontal Clove Hitch, in the order of ① and then ②, wrap the working cord twice around the filler cord. Then, pull each cord in the direction indicated by arrow in the figure on the left.

 *The symbol on the left indicates the knot described in the figure on the left.

**2**

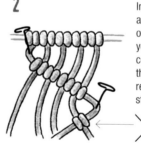

In order to make the knots neat and straight, adjust the angle of the adjacent knot. Once you reach the end of the filler cord, begin again by tying onto the rightmost filler cord and reversing left and right from step 1.

 *The symbol on the left indicates the knot described in the figure on the left.

## Reverse Clove Hitch

Just use the method for tying a Horizontal Clove Hitch (p.8) but reverse the front and back side.

Knot Symbol >>

**1**

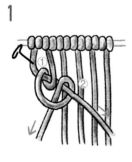

When you wrap the working cord around the filler cord (the leftmost filler cord in the figure), pass the working cord over, then under the filler cord. This creates the first Clove Hitch (①). Next, pass the working cord under, then over the filler cord, to create the second Clove Hitch (②) (reverse Horizontal Clove Hitch).

 *The symbol on the left indicates the knot described in the figure on the left.

**2**

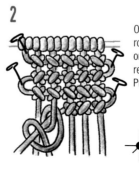

Once you reach the end of the row, move on and begin tying on to the rightmost filler cord reversing left and right in step 1. Proceed to the left.

 *The symbol on the left indicates the knot described in the figure on the left.

## Overhand Knot

This is the most simple knot tying method. Sometimes the knot can be used to put an accent on a pattern. It is also used to prevent fraying.

Knot Symbol >>

**1**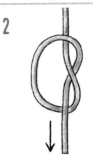

Move the end of the cord following the arrow in the figure above, then through the loop.

**2**

Pull the end to tighten the knot.

**3**

Complete. Even if you use multiple cords at once you tie the knot in the same way.

## Gathering Knot

This method is used to bundle two or more cords with another cord. This knot doesn't become overly cumbersome, even as the number of cords bundled together increases. The finished product will look neat and sharp.

Knot Symbol >>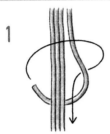

**1**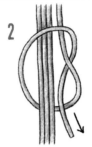

Move the end of the cord following the arrow in the figure above, then pass it through the loop.

**2**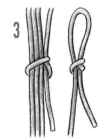

Pull the end to tighten the knot.

**3**

Complete. Even if the number of cords bundled together increases, the knot itself doesn't become too big.

## Sailor's Knot

This is one of the basic knots. It is also called a "Carrick Bend." It hardly ever loosens.

Knot Symbol >>

**1**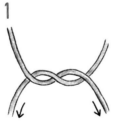

Cross two cords, making two loops, as shown above.

**2**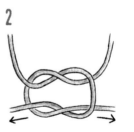

Cross the downward trailing cords as shown above.

**3**

Pull both ends firmly to tighten the knot.

## Wrapping Knot

This is a method for bundling a bunch of cords by wrapping another cord around them. This method is frequently used when bundling many cords at once.

Knot Symbol >>

**1**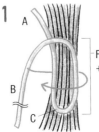

A

Finished size: +0.5cm (¼")

B

C

Fold the working cord and lay it on the filler cords. Then, wrap the working cord around the filler cords. Make sure there are no gaps (see above).

**2**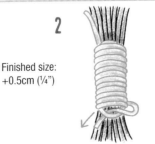

Put the end of B through loop C.

**3**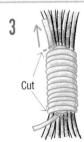

Cut

Pull the end of A so loop C goes under the wrapped binding. Cut off excess A and B.

# Tips for Beginners

This section introduces tips for making your finished product look even more beautiful. These tips will also help you work smoothly and efficiently. Please read this section thoroughly before you start your project.

### TIP 01 Prepare the cords your project requires and sort them

Cut cords to the required length, then sort them into groups. Mark each group using masking tape if you have difficulty finding the cords you need. For example, if your cords are all the same color and material, but their length is different you will want to mark them. Also, you will want to sort your cords into groups and tie them together if you take a break from your project.

### TIP 02 Use a piece of cardboard, or a cord you already cut, for measuring

Some large projects require long cords that are over 5m (16ft.) in length. In such cases, we suggest one of the following.

① Measure the first cord you cut; then, use that cord as a ruler to cut the other cords.

② Prepare a piece of cardboard that has a specific measurement when wrapped once around. Then, use the cardboard to measure and cut cord as needed.

③ When you need an even number of cords, cut two cords at a time.

### TIP 03 Make a skein with a long cord

Long cords are difficult to work with. Coiling a long cord into a small skein in advance prevents the cord from becoming tangled. The picture on the right shows how to make a skein. The point here is to make sure the cord is pulled from inside the skein. Coil even short cords in a small bundle and secure them with an elastic.

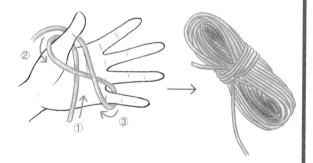

### TIP 04 Avoid or hide a "splice" of cords

Sometimes, there is a "splice" on a long cord due to the manufacturing processes. If there is a splice in your cord just cut off that portion, or try to hide the splice by using the cord as a holding cord, or purposefully position the splice somewhere unnoticeable.

### TIP 05 Tighten the knot uniformly

The more the knots are tightened, the more beautiful the appearance. So, what is the tip for making the knots look uniform? Just be sure to maintain the same amount of force when you tighten the knots and pay attention to the overall look of your project.

### TIP 06 Practice tying knots if you are not sure

"Can I tie this knot?" If you are not sure, practice tying them before you start your project. Keep scraps of cord as they may come in handy for practicing.

## TIP 07
### Use a table to work on small items, hang large items on the wall to work

If your project is small enough to fit on a macramé board, use the board's flat surface to work on your project. Secure the anchor cords using macramé pins. For projects too large or too long to fit on the macramé board, hang them on a hook or a garment rack or put a portion of your project on the macramé board and slide the board along as you progress. Since large sized projects tend to have longer cords, you should suspend them vertically to prevent tangling.

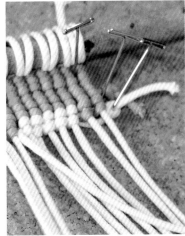 

## TIP 08
### Tying a knot as you confirm its size and position

In order to create knots of a desired size and in a desired position, make frequent measurements and keep everything in order. If you use a macramé board the 1cm ($\frac{3}{8}$") square grid printed on the board comes in handy. If there is no grid printed on the board, make a template using a piece of cardboard (see photo). This will create uniform intervals without the use of a measuring tape.

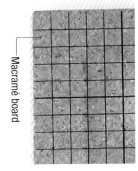

Macramé board

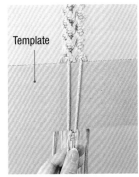

Template

## TIP 09
### Managing ends depending on cord type and knot position

Before trimming the ends of your cords, you need to treat them. There are three different methods for managing ends. There are no strict rules for choosing a method.

Just try to choose one according to the size of the cords, its position, and your general preference.

### A Using a large-eyed sewing needles

Thread a needle with the end of the cord that you need to manage. Then, put the needle through each knot on the backside and cut off the excess. This is the simplest method. As long as the cord has enough length to thread a needle and to make some stitches this method will usually work.

### B Using forceps

This method is used to put the end through a gap using forceps. If the end of the cord easily frays, be sure to apply glue first to prevent fraying. This method is perfect for disposing of thick cord that cannot thread through a needle.

### C Using glue

When you tie the last knot, apply glue to the inside of that knot and tighten to secure. Trim the trailing end very short. You need to buy some glue, but this is the simplest way to manage cord ends.

# CHAPTER
# 01 / Living with Plants

A plant hanger is useful when you don't have enough space for displaying your houseplants. You can make a simple plant hanger within thirty minutes. The benefits of making your own is that you can adjust the length and size based on your potted plants and the space where you intend to hang your plants. Whether houseplants, succulents, or air plants, combine your favorite plants and display them to produce a comfortable atmosphere in your chosen space.

## ITEM A

### Plant Hanger

This plant hanger uses four types of basic knots: The Wrapped Knot, Spiral Knot, Square Knot, and Overhand Knot. This plant hanger has a standard design and is perfect for practicing all of these knots.

Design: Yoshie Ichikawa

## Materials

Natural-color cotton cord (3mm): 23.2m/26yd
cut as follows

ⓐ Working cord: 350cm/12' long, 4 pieces
ⓑ Filler cord: 200cm/7' long, 4 pieces
ⓒ Wrapping cord: 60cm/2' long, 2 pieces
Metal ring: 3cm/1¼" inner diameter

## Techniques

Wrapped Knot (see p.15)
Spiral Knot (see p.9)
Square Knot (see p.10)
Alternating Square Knot (see p.10)
Overhand Knot (see p.15)

Knotting Diagram

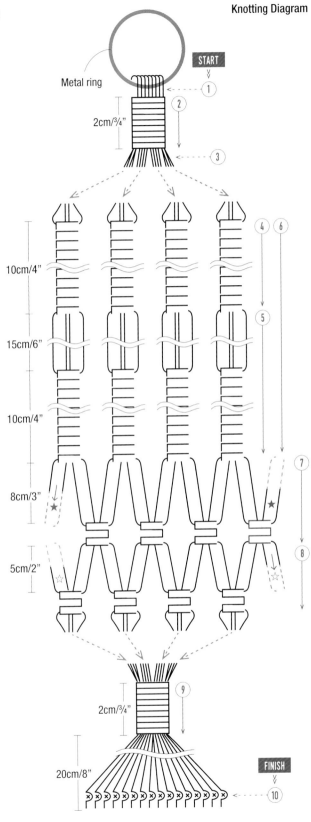

Metal ring

START
① 
2cm/¾"  ②
③
10cm/4"  ④ ⑥
15cm/6"  ⑤
10cm/4"
8cm/3"  ★  ★  ⑦
5cm/2"  ☆  ☆  ⑧
⑨
2cm/¾"
20cm/8"  FINISH
⑩

Next Page ——> **BASIC LESSONS**
Step by step instructions with photographs

21

# BASIC LESSONS:
# Plant Hanger

This is a basic plant hanger made with Spiral Knots and Alternating Square Knots. You can adjust the space between each square knot in order to hang larger or smaller pots. If you want the space between the knots to be equal, prepare a piece of cardboard that is cut to your desired spacing.

*We use three different colored cords for demonstration purposes.

← Watch the tutorial video!
http://www.marchen-art.co.jp/movie/macrame_interior_01

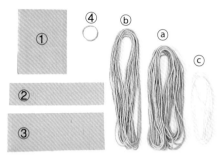

### Preparation

Template: ① 15cm/6" Wide cardboard, ② 5cm/2" Wide cardboard, ③ 8cm/3" Wide cardboard / ④ Metal ring / cords: ⓐ: Working cord 350cm/12' long x 4, ⓑ: Filler cord 200cm/7' long x 4, ⓒ: Wrapping cord 60cm/2' x 2

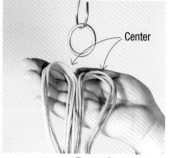

**1**
**-❶**   Fold cords ⓐ and ⓑ in half.

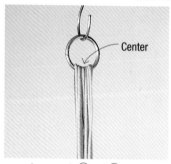

**1**
**-❷**   Loop cords ⓐ and ⓑ through the metal ring hanging on the hook. The middle of the cords are on the ring.

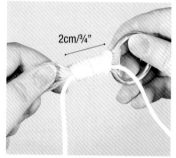

**2**   Take a cord ⓒ and wrap it around below the metal ring. Use it to bundle cords ⓐ and ⓑ. Make this a 2cm/¾" long Wrapped Knot.

**3**   Separate the cords into four groups of four, taking two strands from ⓐ and ⓑ. Tie three groups, bundling each group, and set them aside.

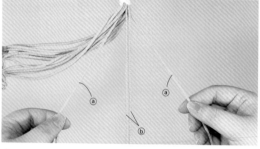

**4**
**-❶**   Take one group that is not bundled and place two strands of ⓑ at the middle. Each strand of ⓐ is on the outside of ⓑ (see picture).

**4**
**-❷**   Make 10cm/4" long Spiral Knots (ⓑ is the filler) from the end of the Wrapped Knot.

**5**
**-❶**   Insert the 15cm/6" wide template below the last Spiral Knot. Place two cords of ⓐ over the template and two cords of ⓑ under the template.

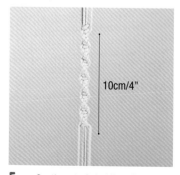

**5**
**-❷**   Continue to Spiral Knot for 10cm/4". You can remove the template after making a few Spiral Knots.

**6** Repeat steps 4 through 5 with the other three groups you set aside. Next, we are going to tie Alternating Square Knots (each knot is two Square Knots) using these four groups to make a tube shape.

**7 -①** Gather two adjoining groups and take the inner four cords. Then, insert the 8cm/3" wide template under ⓑ so that ⓐ is behind the template.

**7 -②** Tie two Square Knots below the template using ⓐ as the filler. Now, one Alternating Square Knot is complete.

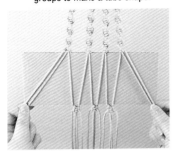

**7 -③** Repeat steps 7-① and 7-② and make two more Alternating Square Knots (tie two Square Knots on each knot). Now, you should have two cords on each side that aren't tied.

**7 -④** Rotate your work so the left side and right side switch places. Remove the template. Insert the template between the cords that are not yet tied and make the last Alternating Square Knot (the red knot symbol in the Knotting Diagram).

**7 -⑤** After tying the last Alternating Square Knot, the first row is complete. Now, the cords form a tubular shape.

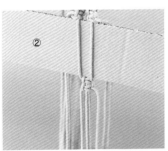

**8 -①** Insert the 5cm/2" template. Tie one row of Alternating Square Knots in the same manner as in step 7 (ⓑ cords are filler and each knot is two Square Knots).

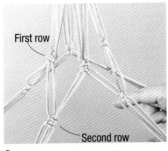

**8 -②** After tying the second row, your cords should look like this (see picture above).

First row

Second row

Complete.

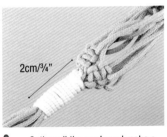

2cm/¾"

**9** Gather all the cords and make a 2cm/¾" long Wrapping Knot below the second row of Alternating Square Knots.

**10** Trim the ends of the cords 20cm/8" from the final row of Alternating Square Knots. Tie an Overhand Knot on each end.

ITEM **B**

Solomon Plant Hanger

ITEM **C**

Net Plant Hanger
INSTRUCTIONS_P.26

ITEM B uses only Square Knot and ITEM C
is made with Overhand Knot. Both begin by
tying from the bottom of the plant hanger.
Design: Märchen Art Studio

24

## Materials

Natural-color cotton cord (3mm): 36.1m/40yd cut as follows
ⓐ Working cord: 500cm/17' long, 4 pieces
ⓑ Working cord: 180cm/6' long, 8 pieces
ⓒ For making a loop: 120cm/4' long, 1 piece
ⓓ For wrapping knots: 50cm/2', 1 piece
Metal ring: 3cm/1¼" diameter
Wood beads: 8 pieces, brown,
date-like shape

## Techniques

Wrapping Knot (see p.15)
Square Knot (see p.10)

## Pot Size

3½-7" top diameter

1  Mount all cord ⓐ and ⓑ on a metal ring (see Cord
Mounting Diagram below and p.8 "Mounting Knot").

2  60cm/2' long ⓑ cord is the filler
cord. Take 120cm/4' long cord ⓑ and
250cm/8'2" long cord ⓐ, both of which
are outside of the filler cord, and make
ten Square Knots. Repeat this step with
the other seven groups of three cords.

3  Gather two sections of Square Knots.
Take the outermost cord on each side
and make two Square Knots using
the four inner cords (ⓐ and ⓑ) as
filler cords. Repeat this step with the
remaining sections.

4  Divide the cords into a group of three,
as in step 2, and tie twelve Square
Knots with each group.

5  Gather two sections of twelve Square
Knots (*skip one section and shift
pairing of subsequent sections). Take
outermost cord ⓐ on each side and
make ten Square Knots using the four
inner cords ⓑ as the filler cord.

6  Pass the four filler cords through a wood bead.

7  Repeat steps 5 through 6 (work on the same sections).

8  Tie twenty-four more Square Knots. Trim the filler cords short.

9  Repeat steps 5 through 8 with subsequent sections.

10  Make a loop for a hook. Refer to "Finishing Up" below.

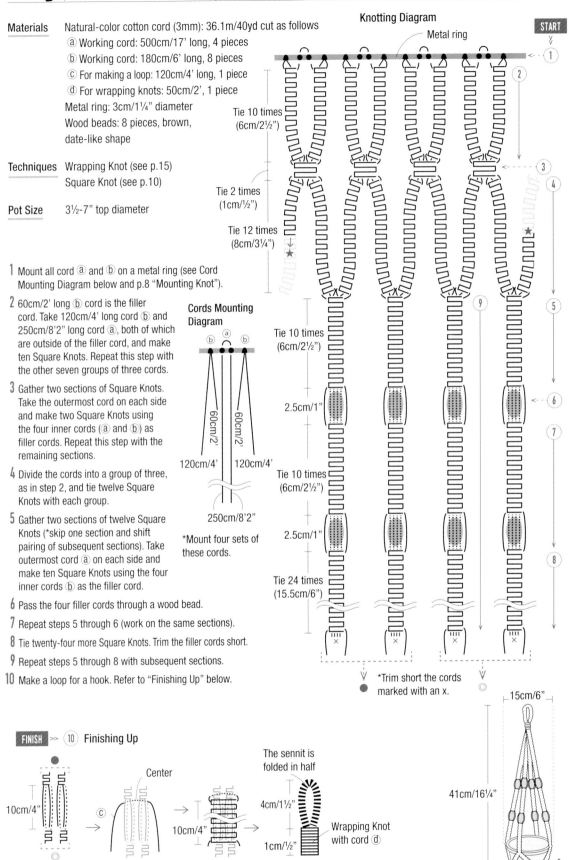

**Knotting Diagram**

Metal ring

START

Tie 10 times
(6cm/2½")

Tie 2 times
(1cm/½")

Tie 12 times
(8cm/3¼")

**Cords Mounting Diagram**

ⓑ  ⓐ  ⓑ

60cm/2'    60cm/2'

120cm/4'    120cm/4'

250cm/8'2"

*Mount four sets of
these cords.

Tie 10 times
(6cm/2½")

2.5cm/1"

Tie 10 times
(6cm/2½")

2.5cm/1"

Tie 24 times
(15.5cm/6")

*Trim short the cords
marked with an x.

15cm/6"

41cm/16¼"

**FINISH** >> ⑩ **Finishing Up**

10cm/4"

As shown above,
join ● and ◎
overlapping by
10cm/4".

Center

Lay ⓒ as shown
above.

10cm/4"

Tie Square Knots
using ⓒ for
10cm/4".

The sennit is
folded in half

4cm/1½"

1cm/½"

Wrapping Knot
with cord ⓓ

Tie Square Knots
using ⓓ for
10cm/4".

25

**Materials**

Natural-color cotton cord (4mm): 29.8m/33yds
cut as follows
ⓐ For Wrapping Knot: 100cm/4' long, 1 piece
ⓑ Working cord: 180cm/6' long, 16 pieces

**Techniques**

Square Knot (see p.10)
Overhand Knot (see p.15)
Wrapping Knot (see p.15)

**Pot Size**

6-8" top diameter

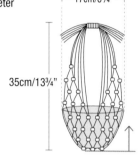

├─17cm/6¾"─┤

35cm/13¾"

1 Bundle all sixteen cords of ⓑ. At the center of the bundle, tie one and a half Square Knots. Use the outermost two cords on each side as the working cords and the rest of the twelve cords as filler cords (see p.27 "Starting Knots").

2 Divide the cords into a group of two cords. On each group, move down 2cm/¾" from the Square Knot you tied in step 1, and tie one Overhand Knot (row 1, tie sixteen times in total).

3 Shift the pairing of the two cords by one. On each group of two cords, move down 2.5cm/1" and tie one Overhand Knot (row 2).

4 Repeat step 3 to tie from rows 3 through 5.

5 Divide the cords into two equal groups on row 6. Leaving the outermost cord on each side, tie an Overhand Knot that is the same as the previous row.

6 In a similar manner to step 5, tie Overhand Knots until you reach row 10 while skipping the outermost cord on each side on each row.

7 Gather the cords of each group.

8 Refer to the "Finishing Up" section below to bundle the two group of cords.

**Knotting Diagram ❶**

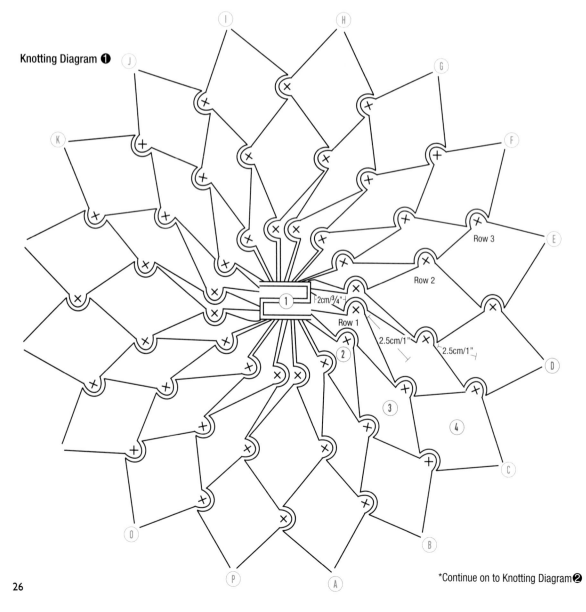

*Continue on to Knotting Diagram ❷

## Knotting Diagram ❷

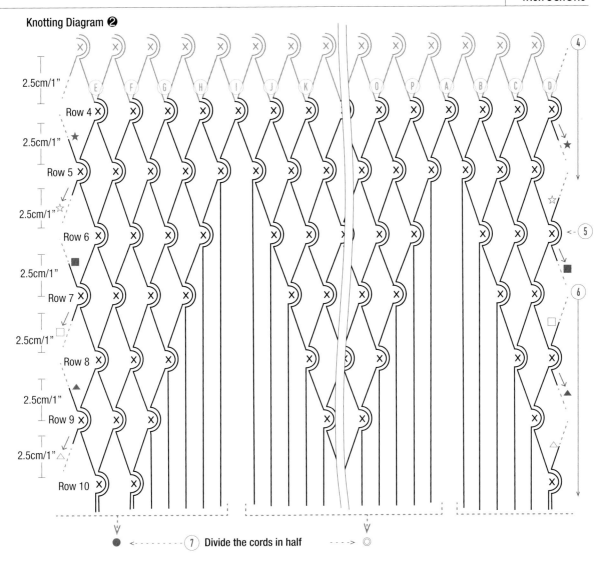

Divide the cords in half

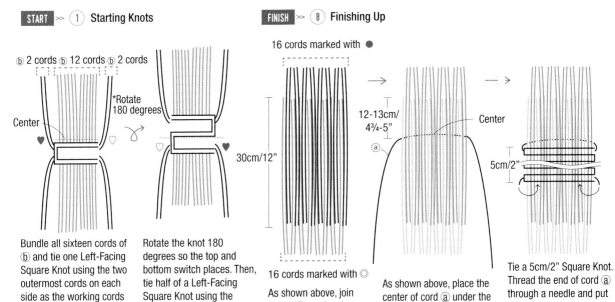

**START** ≫ ① Starting Knots

ⓑ 2 cords ⓑ 12 cords ⓑ 2 cords

Center

*Rotate 180 degrees

Bundle all sixteen cords of ⓑ and tie one Left-Facing Square Knot using the two outermost cords on each side as the working cords and remaining twelve cords as the filler cords.

Rotate the knot 180 degrees so the top and bottom switch places. Then, tie half of a Left-Facing Square Knot using the cords marked with ♥ and ♡ (see diagram above). Now, the centers of the cords are knotted.

**FINISH** ≫ ⑧ Finishing Up

16 cords marked with ●

30cm/12"

16 cords marked with ◎

As shown above, join ● and ◎ overlapping 30cm/12".

12-13cm/ 4¾-5"

Center

ⓐ

As shown above, place the center of cord ⓐ under the bundle.

5cm/2"

Tie a 5cm/2" Square Knot. Thread the end of cord ⓐ through a needle and put the cord under the Square Knot to hide it.

## ITEM D

### Flat Pocket Plant Hanger
INSTRUCTIONS_P.30

This is a tapestry-like plant hanger. Enjoy the beauty of both the macramé pattern and the plants at the same time.

Design: Etsuko Usami

## ITEM E

### Pocket Plant Hanger
INSTRUCTIONS_P.31

This is a simple and snug wall-hanging plant hanger. All you need is a hook on the wall to display.

Design: Etsuko Usami

**Materials**
Natural-color cotton cord (3mm): 29m/32yd cut as follows
ⓐ 200cm/7' long , 14 pieces
ⓑ For Wrapping Knots: 50cm/2' long ,1 piece
ⓒ Hanging loop: 50cm/2' long, 1 piece
Wood piece: 1 piece

**Techniques**
Square Knot (see p.10) / Alternating Square Knots (see p.10) /
Wrapping Knot (see p.15) / Overhand Knot (see p.15)

**Pot Size**
3½" top diameter

1 Fold ⓐ in half and mount to the wood piece. Mount all fourteen cords of ⓐ (see p.8, "Mounting Knots").

2 Tie one Square Knot on each group of four cords.

3 For the next three rows, tie Alternating Square Knots. Leave 1.5cm/½" spaces between each row.

4 For the next three rows, use fourteen cords on the right-side and tie Alternating Square Knots. For each row, skip the two leftmost cords.

5 Do the same with the fourteen cords on the left-side. But, skip the two rightmost cords in each row.

6 Now, you should have twelve cords at the center that are not tied. Take the two outermost cords on each side and tie one Square Knot with the inner eight cords as the filler cords.

7 The next three rows use fourteen cords on the right-side and tie Alternating Square Knots. Do not skip any cords.

8 Do the same as in step 7 using fourteen cords on the left-side.

9 Tie a row of Alternating Square Knots.

10 Move down 4cm/1½". For the next two rows, tie Alternating Square Knots (tie one-and-half Square Knots on each knot). (After tying the red Knot Symbol, the circle will be closed.)

11 Gather all the cords (twenty-eight) and tie a Wrapping Knot 4cm/1½" below the last Square Knot.

12 Trim the ends of the cords 20cm/8" down from the last Square Knot. Attach cord ⓒ to each end of the wood piece to complete.

**Knotting Diagram**

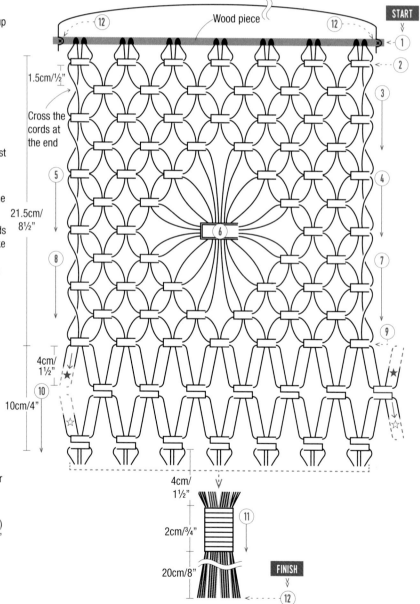

1.5cm/½"

Cross the cords at the end

21.5cm/ 8½"

Wood piece

4cm/ 1½"

10cm/4"

4cm/ 1½"

2cm/¾"

20cm/8"

**Materials**
Natural-color cotton cord (2mm): 16.5m/19yds,
cut as follows:
ⓐ Working cord: 200cm/7' long, 8 pieces
ⓑ For Wrapping Knots: 50cm/2' long, 1 piece
Wooden ring: 44mm/1¾" outer diameter, 1 piece
Natural wood bead

**Techniques**
Square Knot (see p.10)
Alternating Square Knots (see p.10)
Spiral Knot (see p.9)
Wrapping Knot (see p.15)

**Pot Size**
3½-6" top diameter

### How to Thread a Wood Bead

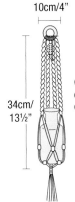

Wood bead

### Knotting Diagram

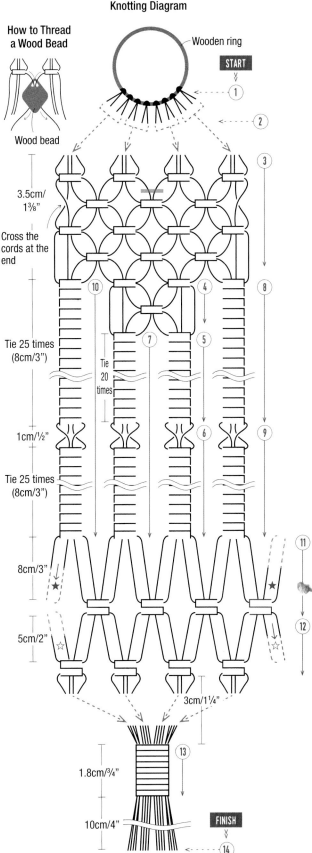

1 Fold cord ⓐ in half and mount on the wooden ring. Mount all eight cords of ⓐ (see p.8, "Mounting Knots").

2 Divide the cords into groups of four cords from the outermost.

3 Tie Alternating Square Knots for row 1 to row 4 (each knot is one Square Knot) on each group. Thread a wooden bead at the spot marked with a brown bar (see Knotting Diagram).

4 Use the inner eight cords to tie Alternating Square Knots (each knot is one Square Knot) for the next two rows.

5 Take four cords from the inner eight cords on the right and tie twenty Right-Twisted Spiral Knots. Of those four cords, the two inner cords are the filler and the cords on each side are the working cords.

6 Switch the filler and the working cords. Move down 1cm/½" and tie twenty-five Right-Twisted Spiral Knots.

7 Take four cords from the inner eight cords on the left. Then, repeat steps 5 through 6 but tie Left-Twisted Spiral Knots.

8 Take four cords from the rightmost edge and tie twenty-five Right-Twisted Spiral Knots. The inner two cords are the filler and the cords on each side are the working cords.

9 Switch the filler and the working cords. Move down 1cm/½" and tie twenty-five Right-Twisted Spiral Knots.

10 Take four cords from leftmost edge. Repeat steps 8 through 9, but this time tie Left-Twisted Spiral Knots.

11 Move down 8cm/3" and tie one row of Alternating Square Knots (each knot is one-and-a-half Square Knots). (After tying the red Knot Symbol, the circle is closed.)

12 Move down 5cm/2" and tie one row of Alternating Square Knots (each knot is one-and-a-half Square Knot).

13 Gather all the cords (sixteen) and tie a Wrapping Knot 3cm/1" below the last Square Knot.

14 Trim the ends of the cords 10cm/4" down from the final knot to complete.

31

## Double-Decker Plant Hanger
### INSTRUCTIONS_P.34

This is a two-tiered plant hanger that effectively uses the rough textures of thick jute. It has a certain presence that creates a focal point in your chosen space.

Design: Märchen Art Studio

## Canopy Plant Hanger
### INSTRUCTIONS_P.36

This is a popular canopy-style plant hanger. Use of the natural-color jute cord produces the subtle and delicate look of the plant hanger.

Design: anudo

## Materials

White jute cord (thick): 50m/55yards
  ⓐ Working cord: 600cm/20' long,
    8 pieces
  ⓑ For Wrapping Knot: 100cm/4' long,
    2 pieces
Metal ring
3cm (1¼") diameter: 1 piece
5cm (2") diameter: 1 piece

## Techniques

Square Knot (see p.10)
Alternating Square Knots (see p.10)
Wrapping Knot (see p.15)
Overhand Knot (see p.15)

## Pot Size

Top tier: 5-7" top diameter
Bottom tier: 8-10½" top diameter

1 Mount all eight ⓐ on a metal ring (3cm/1¼"
diameter). (See p.8, "Mounting Knots.")

2 Divide ⓐ into a group of four cords and tie two Square
Knots in each group.

3 Move down 5cm/2" and tie Alternating Square Knots
(two on each group) for one row (after tying the red Knot
Symbol, see Knotting Diagram, the circle is closed).

4 Move down 10cm/4" and tie one row of Alternating
Square Knots (tie two on each group).

5 Skip two cords and take four subsequent cords. Move
down 12cm/4¾" and tie Square Knots for 30cm/11¾".

6 Take four cords to the left of the Spiral Knots you tied
in step 5. Move down 12cm/4¾" from the knots tied in
step 4 and tie Spiral Knots for 30cm/11¾".

7 Repeat steps 5 through 6 with the remaining eight
cords.

8 Gather all sixteen cords and tie Wrapping Knots with
one cord ⓑ.

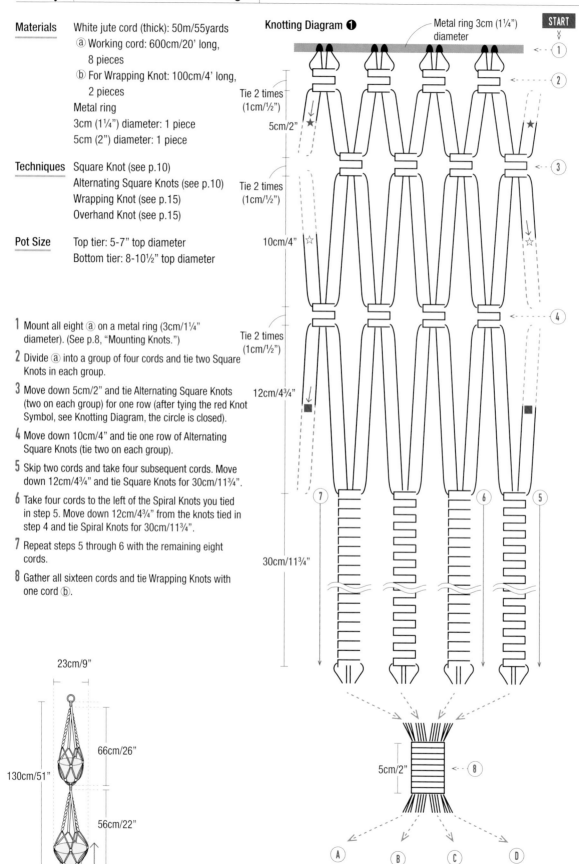

Knotting Diagram ❶

Metal ring 3cm (1¼")
diameter

START

Tie 2 times
(1cm/½")

5cm/2"

Tie 2 times
(1cm/½")

10cm/4"

Tie 2 times
(1cm/½")

12cm/4¾"

30cm/11¾"

23cm/9"

66cm/26"

130cm/51"

56cm/22"

5cm/2"

*Continue with Knotting Diagram ❷

Knotting Diagram ❷

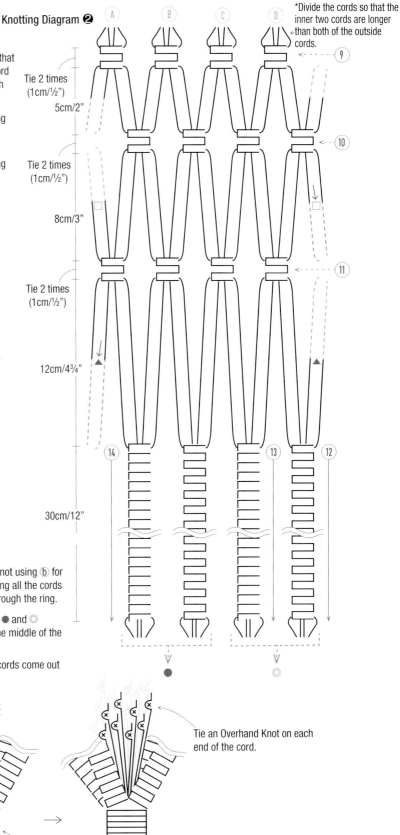

*Divide the cords so that the inner two cords are longer than both of the outside cords.

9 Divide the cords again into groups of four cords that have two long cords on the inside and a short cord on each side. Then, tie two Square Knots on each group.

10 Move down 5cm/2" and tie one row of Alternating Square Knots (tie two Square Knots on each group).

11 Move down 8cm/3" and tie one row of Alternating Square Knots (tie two Square Knots on each group).

12 Skip two cords and take the subsequent four cords. Move down 12cm/4¾" and tie Square Knots for 30cm/11¾".

13 Take the four cords left to the Square Knots you tied in step 12. Move down 12cm/4¾" from the knots tied in step 11 and tie Spiral Knots for 30cm/11¾".

14 Repeat steps 12 through 13 with the remaining eight cords.

15 Refer to "Finishing Up." Tie ⓐ with a Wrapping Knot using ⓑ and tie an Overhand Knot with the ends of ⓐ to complete.

Tie 2 times (1cm/½")
5cm/2"

Tie 2 times (1cm/½")
8cm/3"

Tie 2 times (1cm/½")
12cm/4¾"

30cm/12"

FINISH >> 15 Finishing Up

Thread ● and ◎ through to the metal ring as shown below. The ring comes to 4cm/1½" below the last knot on both ● and ◎.

Tie a Wrapping Knot using ⓑ for 4cm/1½", bundling all the cords and threading through the ring.

The ends of both ● and ◎ come out from the middle of the Wrapping Knot.

The ends of the cords come out from the middle.

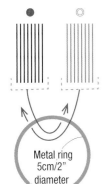

Metal ring 5cm/2" diameter

4cm/1½"

Wrapping Knot with ⓑ

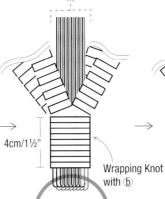

Tie an Overhand Knot on each end of the cord.

# ITEM G | Canopy Plant Hanger | PHOTO_P.32

**Materials**

Natural-color jute cord (thick): 111m/122yds cut as follows

ⓐ Working cord: 600cm/20' long, 12 pieces
ⓑ Working cord: 300cm/10' long, 12 pieces
ⓒ For Wrapping Knot: 100cm/4' long, 1 piece
ⓓ For Wrapping Knot: 150cm/5' long, 1 piece
Metal ring: 13cm/5" diameter, 2 pieces
Metal ring: 23cm/9" diameter, 1 piece

**Techniques**

Square Knot (see p.10) / Wrapping Knot (see p.15) /
Alternating Square Knots (see p.10) / Horizontal Clove Hitch
(see p.8) / Spiral Knot (see p.9) / Vertical Lark's Head Knot
(see p.12) / Diagonal Clove Hitch (see p.14)

**Pot Size**

7–9½" top diameter

**Knotting Diagram ❶**

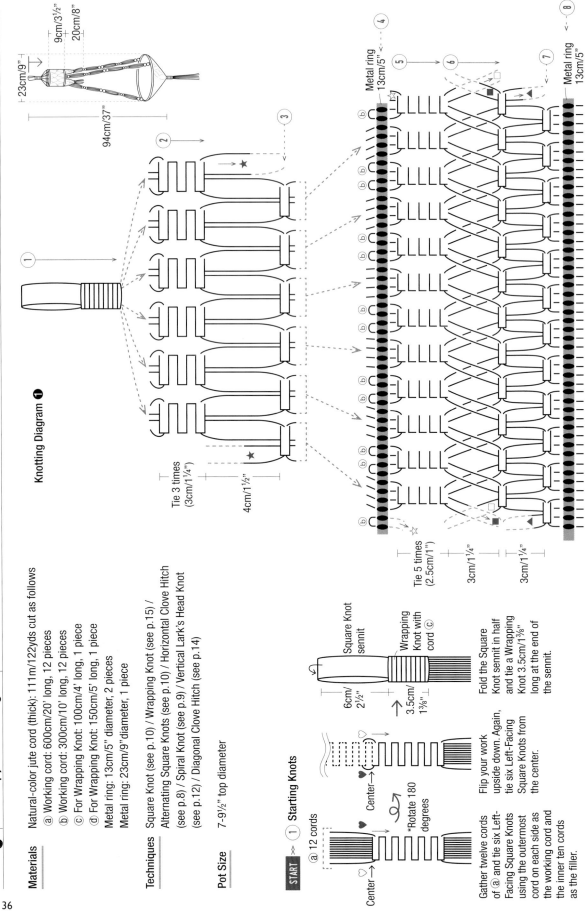

**START >> ① Starting Knots**

ⓐ 12 cords

Gather twelve cords of ⓐ and tie six Left-Facing Square Knots using the outermost cord on each side as the working cord and the inner ten cords as the filler.

*Rotate 180 degrees

Flip your work upside down. Again, tie six Left-Facing Square Knots from the center.

Square Knot sennit

Wrapping Knot with cord ⓒ

6cm/2½"
3.5cm/1⅜"

Fold the Square Knot sennit in half and tie a Wrapping Knot 3.5cm/1⅜" long at the end of the sennit.

Tie 3 times (3cm/1¼")

4cm/1½"

Metal ring 13cm/5"

Tie 5 times (2.5cm/1")

3cm/1¼"

3cm/1¼"

Metal ring 13cm/5"

23cm/9"
9cm/3½"
20cm/8"
94cm/37"

36

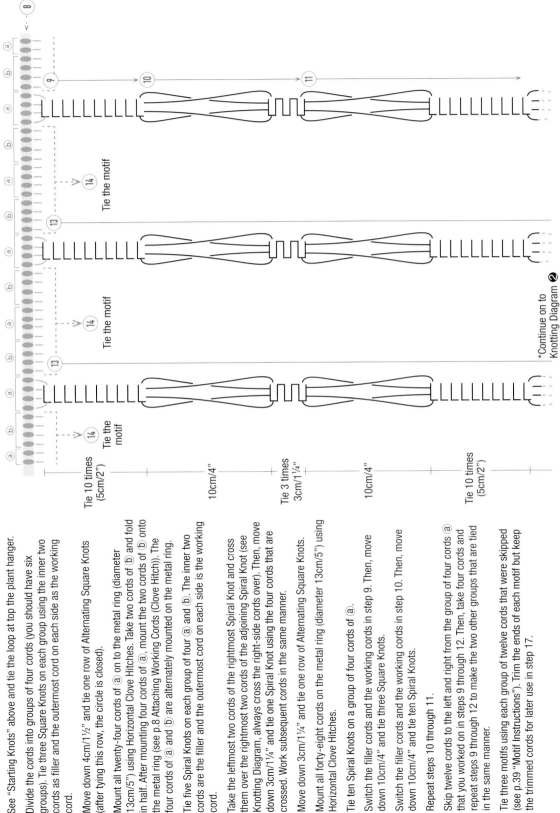

*Allocation of the cords ⓐ and ⓑ after completing step 8.

Tie the motif

Tie the motif

Tie the motif

Tie 10 times (5cm/2")

10cm/4"

Tie 3 times 3cm/1¼"

10cm/4"

Tie 10 times (5cm/2")

*Continue on to Knotting Diagram ❷

1 See "Starting Knots" above and tie the loop at top the plant hanger.

2 Divide the cords into groups of four cords (you should have six groups). Tie three Square Knots on each group using the inner two cords as filler and the outermost cord on each side as the working cord.

3 Move down 4cm/1½" and tie one row of Alternating Square Knots (after tying this row, the circle is closed).

4 Mount all twenty-four cords of ⓐ on to the metal ring (diameter 13cm/5") using Horizontal Clove Hitches. Take two cords of ⓑ and fold in half. After mounting four cords of ⓐ, mount the two cords of ⓑ onto the metal ring (see p.8 Attaching Working Cords (Clove Hitch). The four cords of ⓐ and ⓑ are alternately mounted on the metal ring.

5 Tie five Spiral Knots on each group of four ⓐ and ⓑ. The inner two cords are the filler and the outermost cord on each side is the working cord.

6 Take the leftmost two cords of the rightmost Spiral Knot and cross them over the rightmost two cords of the adjoining Spiral Knot (see Knotting Diagram, always cross the right-side cords over). Then, move down 3cm/1¼" and tie the one Spiral Knot using the four cords that are crossed. Work subsequent cords in the same manner.

7 Move down 3cm/1¼" and tie one row of Alternating Square Knots.

8 Mount all forty-eight cords on the metal ring (diameter 13cm/5") using Horizontal Clove Hitches.

9 Tie ten Spiral Knots on a group of four cords of ⓐ.

10 Switch the filler cords and the working cords in step 9. Then, move down 10cm/4" and tie the three Square Knots.

11 Switch the filler cords and the working cords in step 10. Then, move down 10cm/4" and tie the ten Spiral Knots.

12 Repeat steps 10 through 11.

13 Skip twelve cords to the left and right from the group of four cords ⓐ that you worked on in steps 9 through 12. Then, take four cords and repeat steps 9 through 12 to make the two other groups that are tied in the same manner.

14 Tie three motifs using each group of twelve cords that were skipped (see p.39 "Motif Instructions"). Trim the ends of each motif but keep the trimmed cords for later use in step 17.

37

## Knotting Diagram ❷

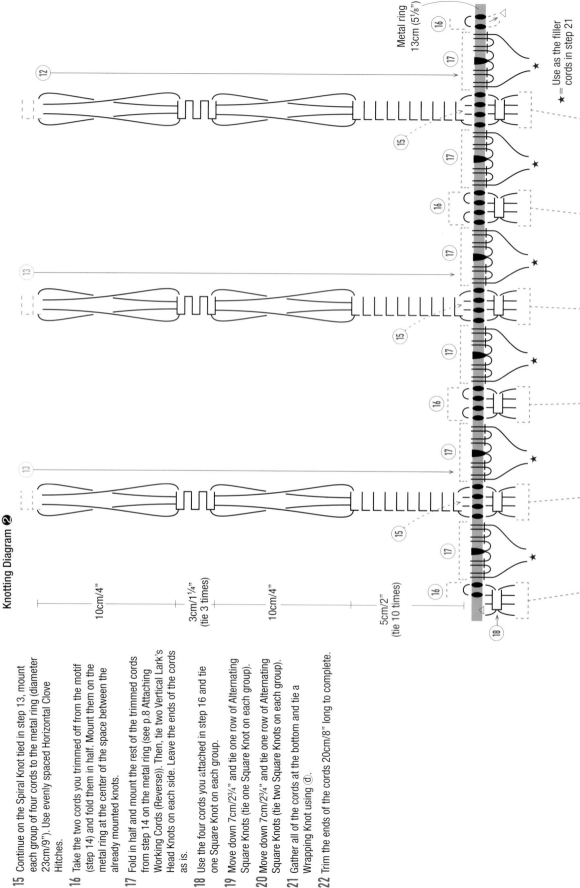

Metal ring
13cm (5⅛")

★ = Use as the filler
cords in step 21

10cm/4"

3cm/1¼"
(tie 3 times)

10cm/4"

5cm/2"
(tie 10 times)

15 Continue on the Spiral Knot tied in step 13, mount each group of four cords to the metal ring (diameter 23cm/9"). Use evenly spaced Horizontal Clove Hitches.

16 Take the two cords you trimmed off from the motif (step 14) and fold them in half. Mount them on the metal ring at the center of the space between the already mounted knots.

17 Fold in half and mount the rest of the trimmed cords from step 14 on the metal ring (see p.8 Attaching Working Cords (Reverse)). Then, tie two Vertical Lark's Head Knots on each side. Leave the ends of the cords as is.

18 Use the four cords you attached in step 16 and tie one Square Knot on each group.

19 Move down 7cm/2¾" and tie one row of Alternating Square Knots (tie one Square Knot on each group).

20 Move down 7cm/2¾" and tie one row of Alternating Square Knots (tie two Square Knots on each group).

21 Gather all of the cords at the bottom and tie a Wrapping Knot using ⓓ.

22 Trim the ends of the cords 20cm/8" long to complete.

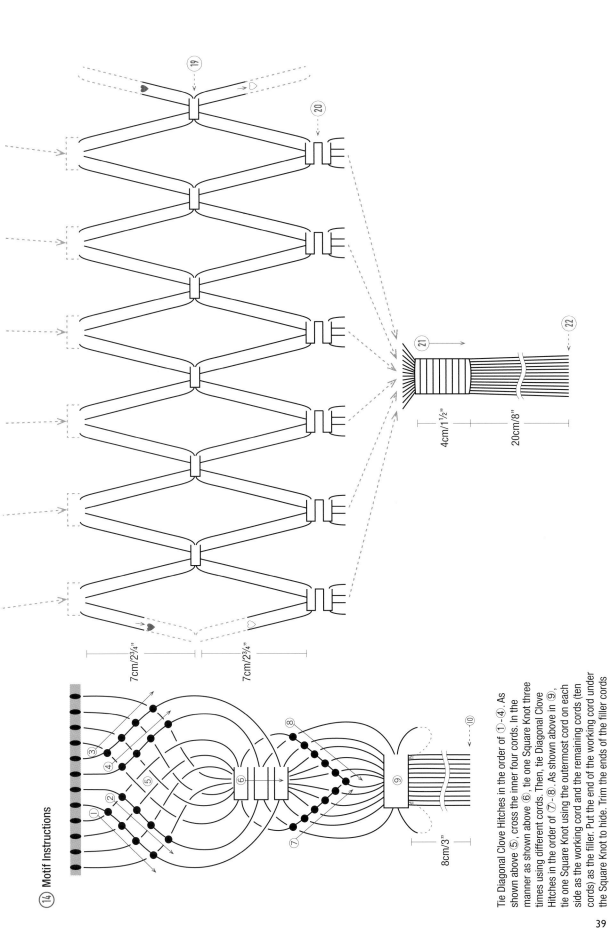

## ⑭ Motif Instructions

7cm/2³/₄"

7cm/2³/₄"

8cm/3"

4cm/1¹/₂"

20cm/8"

Tie Diagonal Clove Hitches in the order of ①-④. As shown above ⑤, cross the inner four cords. In the manner as shown above ⑥, tie one Square Knot three times using different cords. Then, tie Diagonal Clove Hitches in the order of ⑦-⑧. As shown above in ⑨, tie one Square Knot using the outermost cord on each side as the working cord and the remaining cords (ten cords) as the filler. Put the end of the working cord under the Square Knot to hide. Trim the ends of the filler cords 8cm/3" long to complete (⑩). Keep the trimmed ends for step 17.

39

# Tips to Enjoy Hanging Displays

Text: Kanae Ishii

Even though you wish to incorporate hanging displays in your décor, surprisingly there are things that you are not sure of or that you find difficult to decide upon. Like, choosing the best place for the hanging display or which plants to select. I would like to share with you a few fail-safe tips for enjoying stylish hanging displays.

## TIPS_01　Properly use "suspended-type" and "hanging-type" displays

The plant hangers are roughly divided into two types, "suspended-type" that hang down from the ceiling and "hanging-type" that are hooked on the wall.

### ①Suspended-type
The charm of this type of display is that you can see the plants from 360 degrees. Installing a hook is required if you wish to suspend the plant hanger from the ceiling. Instead of installing a hook on the ceiling, you can use a curtain rod or garment rack or coat hanger. The benefit of using a garment rack or a coat hanger is that you can easily move it when you want to display your plants somewhere else.

### ②Hanging-type
This type is casual and doesn't take up much space because it hangs anywhere there is a wall. It is just like a tapestry. You need to install a hook on the wall of course. However, sometimes you can use masking tape to secure the plant hanger if it is light enough. The hanging-type can be enjoyed almost anywhere, it all depends on the layout and environment of your chosen space.

Suspended-type: Use a chain hook to adjust the height when it is suspended from the ceiling.

Hanging-type: Versatile and easy to adjust the height.

## TIPS_02　Choose plants suitable for a hanging display

Hanging displays provide superior airflow, but the soil also dries easily. Which is to say, drought resistant plants are most suitable for hanging displays. For example, cacti, succulents and other drought resistant plants. Air plants, like Tillandsia, can be given a spritz of water and don't need soil. So, considering its lightweight, Tillandsia is perfect for a hanging display. Also, considering the fact that the display is hung up high, drooping vines and plants that grow downwards are most suitable. Hanging displays solve your problems for choosing a place to display these types of plants and you can enjoy the view. It will be as if green vines are floating in the air.

Left: Air plants can be hung like this.
Top: Hanging displays allow you to fully enjoy drooping vines.

**Be playful with pots**

One thing you need to think about when undertaking hanging displays is to prevent water spillage. Hang potted plants (including the saucer), put a plant pot in a cover and then hang, etc. If you have a plan in place for water spillage, you can enjoy hanging displays anytime you desire. Various types of plant containers are commercially available so just choose the one that goes well with your interior décor and the plant you intend to use.

The only difference between a plant pot and plant container is whether there is a drain hole or not. You can use a dish, bowl, empty can/bottle, or a cooking pot for your plant container. Be playful and enjoy your display. But, don't forget to drain any excess water when you use a plant container to prevent rotting roots.

Also, you can enjoy hanging displays of cut flowers in a vase or air plants instead of potted plants. Hanging displays are very versatile.

Use a wooden salad bowl as a plant container. It's light and charming.

Put air plants in a glass bowl and enjoy a clear hanging display. The glass container lets you to see inside. It also makes caring for the plants easier.

## TIPS_04  **Decide on the focal point of your layout**

Your first priority when choosing a space for your hanging display is to consider sun light and airflow suitable for your plants. Also, take the following points into account when choosing plants and areas as part of your interior décor.

### ①Fill white space
Suitable heights for hanging display tend to be "white space" because very little furniture will reach up high. Hang your plants so as to fill such white space. This will harmonize your space.

### ②Hang one large piece
The two tiered and canopy-style plant hangers introduced on p.32 are large. They are over 1m/4' tall, including fringes. Thus, they have a certain presence and act like a piece of furniture. Use these large pieces as a partition in a room to blend in with other interior décor items.

### ③Hang multiple small to medium sized plant hangers of varying height and depth
I would recommend hanging multiple small to medium sized plant hangers that vary in height and depth. Display them in layers and with depth to create rhythm and give off a vibrant feel within your chosen space. Not only is this visually pleasing, it also makes your space look more open.

Besides hanging multiple plants, try to incorporate other interior décor items to create certain rhythms in your chosen space.

CHAPTER

02

# Wall Decoration

Simply hanging a small tapestry will dictate your style of interior décor or harmonize the overall décor of a certain space. After a plant hanger, a macramé tapestry is the item we encourage you to try for your next project. Pattern and depth variety created by macramé tapestries will surely please your eye.

## ITEM H

**Vertical Clove Hitch Tapestry**

"Vertical Clove Hitch Work" creates patterns. Let's create a colorful Native American motif tapestry.

Design: Miyuki Ozaki

## Materials

Cotton cord (3mm)
- ⓐ Natural-color: 36.6m/41yds long
- ⓑ Orange-color: 8.1m/9yds long
- ⓒ Gray-color: 38m/42yds long
- ⓓ Black-color: 25m/28yds long

Natural wood piece: 3cm/1¼" inner diameter, 1 piece

## Techniques

Vertical Clove Hitch (p.14) / Overhand Knot (see p.15)

## Cord Length

| Color | Use | Cord Length | Need |
|---|---|---|---|
| Cord ⓐ 3mm | Filler cord | 100cm/4' | 24 pcs |
| | Filler cord | 60cm/2' | 1 pcs |
| | Working cord | 100cm/4' | 4 pcs |
| | Working cord | 7m/23' | 1 pcs |
| | Hanging loop | 100cm/4' | 1 pcs |
| Cord ⓑ | Working cord | 340cm/11'2" | 2 pcs |
| | Working cord | 130cm/4'3" | 1 pcs |
| Cord ⓒ | Working cord | 19m/62'4" | 2 pcs |
| Cord ⓓ | Working cord | 13m/42'8" | 1 pcs |
| | Working cord | 12m/29'4" | 1 pcs |

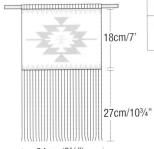

18cm/7'

27cm/10¾"

24cm (9½")

## Knotting Diagram

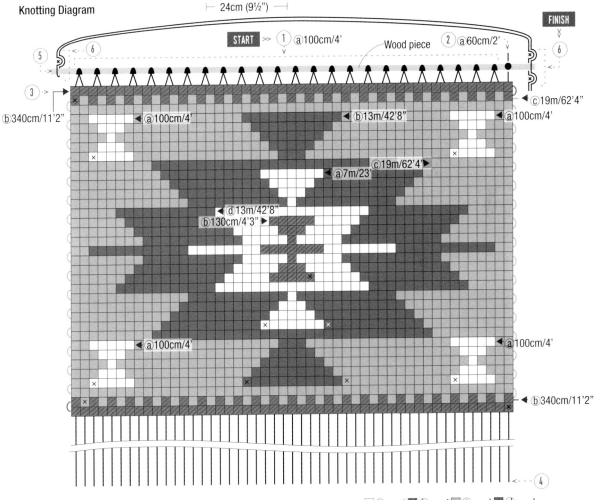

- ☐ Vertical Clove Hitch
- ► Change color

After tying a knot, marked with ×, trim off the cord.

☐ ⓐ cord ▨ ⓑ cord ▧ ⓒ cord ■ ⓓ cord

Next Page ——— BASIC LESSONS

Step by step instructions with photographs

# BASIC LESSONS:
## Vertical Clove Hitch Tapestry

"Vertical Clove Hitch Work" is a method for creating patterns using Vertical Clove Hitches. The key points here are adding different colored cords, how to attach cords when changing them, as well as how to hide a cord after you finished tying knots. This section will provide instructions for making the tapestry as well as introducing the basics of Vertical Clove Hitch Work.

◀ Watch the tutorial video!
http://www.marchen-art.co.jp/movie/macrame_interior_02

**1** Fold cord ⓐ in half and mount it to the wood piece using a "Basic Mounting Knots" (see p.8). Mount all twenty-four cords of ⓐ.

### Basics of Vertical Clove Hitch Work

**2** Mount the 60cm/2' long cord ⓐ on the wood piece at the rightmost position using a Horizontal Clove Hitch (see p.8).

**3-❶** On the leftmost cord ⓐ, attach the 340cm/11'2" long cord ⓑ and tie a Vertical Clove Hitch. Then, work on subsequent cords of ⓐ.

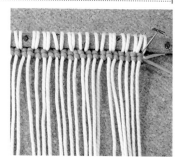

**3-❷** For row 1, tie a Vertical Clove Hitch with cord ⓑ. Tie each knot without a gap.

### Adding a cord ▶

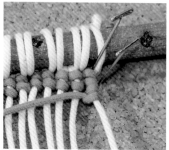

**3-❸** Begin row 2. Move cord ⓑ back to the left and then tie one Vertical Clove Hitch.

**3-❹** Under cord ⓑ, add the 14m/46' long cord ⓒ and tie the first loop of the Vertical Clove Hitch on the next filler cord.

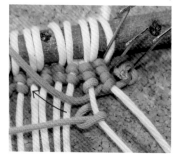

**3-❺** Pull the working end of cord ⓑ over and tie the second loop of your Vertical Clove Hitch with cord ⓒ, just below the cord ⓑ.

### Change Color

**3-❻** The next knot uses cord ⓑ. In a similar manner to steps 3-❹ and 3-❺, put cord ⓒ under the filler cord and tie one Vertical Clove Hitch with cord ⓑ. Place cord ⓒ between the two loops of the knot.

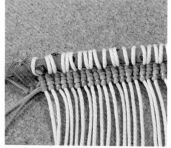

**3-❼** Alternating cords ⓑ and ⓒ, tie Vertical Clove Hitches on end of row 2.

### Hiding the cord x

**3-❽** Turn your work over, weave the end of cord ⓑ inside a few knots using a needle but be sure to skip the first knot. Dispose any excess of ⓑ.

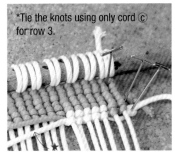

*Tie the knots using only cord ⓒ for row 3.

3 -❾ Begin row 4. After making one knot each on the first two filler cords with cord ⓒ, add the 80cm/2'8" long cord ⓐ (★, photo above) and tie one Vertical Clove Hitch each on the next five filler cords.

3 -❿ Move the working end of cord ⓐ (★, photo above) down to set it aside. Continue to tie ⓒ to the subsequent filler cords.

3 -⓫ As specified in the Knotting Diagram, add a cord to change color (just as you did in steps 3-❾ and 3-❿). Continue to work on row 4.

Moving row ·······················································

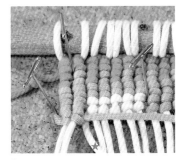

3 -⓬ Begin row 5. Tie one Vertical Clove Hitch on each of the first two filler cords (★ is cord ⓐ that you set aside in row 4).

3 -⓭ Tie one Vertical Clove Hitch while placing the working end of cord ⓐ (★) between the loop of the knot (move cord ⓐ where you need it by inserting the cord between the loops).

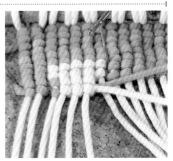

3 -⓮ Switch places with cords ⓒ and ⓐ. Tie one Vertical Clove Hitch each on the next three filler cords inserting cord ⓒ between the loops of the knot.

3 -⓯ As specified in the Knotting Diagram, add a cord to change colors (as you did in steps 3-⓭ and 3-⓮). Continue to work on row 5.

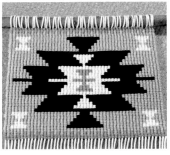

3 -⓰ From row 6 onward, work until you reach row 35 in a manner similar to steps 3-❶ through 3-⓯.

4 Trim the ends of the filler cords to the desired length.

5 Attach a cord to make a hanger. Fold the 100cm/4' long cord ⓐ in half. Insert the left end of the wood piece in a loop of cord ⓐ and tie an Overhand Knot.

6 -❶ Tie another Overhand Knot 15cm/6" inside from the other end of cord ⓐ.

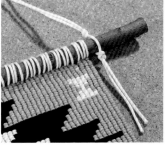

6 -❷ Insert the right end of the wood below the knot and tie an Overhand Knot once again to complete.

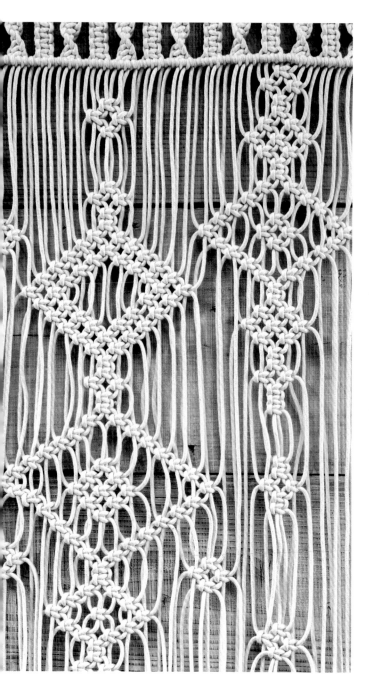

ITEM 1

**Diamond-Shaped Pattern Tapestry**
INSTRUCTIONS_P.50

The design of this tapestry is made with diamond-shapes using Alternating Square Knots. The key points for creating symmetrical patterns is to make the knots level along the horizontal axis.

Design: Aki Hagino

**Materials**

Natural-color cotton cord (3mm):
Approx. 142m/156yds long
ⓐ Working cord: 390cm/13' long, 36 pieces
ⓑ Filler cord: 50cm/2' long, 2 pieces
ⓒ Hanging loop: 1 piece, length as desired
Tapestry rod: 40cm/15¾", 1 piece

**Techniques**

Horizontal Clove Hitch (see p.8)
Square Knot (see p.10)
Alternating Square Knots (see p.10)

1 Fold a piece of cord ⓐ in half and mount it on a tapestry rod. Mount all thirty-six cords (see p.8 "Mounting Knot (Double)").

2 Select a 50cm/2' long cord ⓑ (tie Overhand Knot at the end and pin it down). Tie one row of Horizontal Clove Hitches with cord ⓑ from the leftmost ⓐ.

3 From the leftmost edge take four cords of ⓐ. Tie eight Square Knots with the outermost cord on each side using the inner two cords as filler. Take the next four cords of ⓐ and tie fourteen Spiral Knots with the outermost cord on each side using the inner two cords as filler. Repeat step 3 eight more times using subsequent ⓐ cords.

4 Tie a row of Horizontal Clove Hitches in a similar manner to step 2.

5 Tie Pattern A. Take eight cords of ⓐ from the center. Move down 2cm/¾" and tie knots to make the pattern marked with a ★. Follow the Knotting Diagram and tie knots as specified. Be sure to leave the space specified in the Knotting Diagram between the knots. (If no spacing is specified, do not leave any gaps between the knots. However, to make nice diamond-shaped patterns, allow some space between the knots).

6 Refer to the Knotting Diagram to make Pattern B. Be sure to leave space between the knots if specified. As seen in Pattern B, begin with the eleventh through fourteenth cords of ⓐ from the left. As seen in Pattern B, begin with the eleventh through fourteenth cords of ⓐ from the right.

7 Again, refer to the Knotting Diagram and tie knots to make Pattern C found below Pattern A.

8 Trim the ends of ⓐ to the desired length.

9 Hide the ends of both ⓑ cords used in steps 2 and 4 (see "Hiding Cords" below). Attach a hanging cord to both ends of the rod to complete.

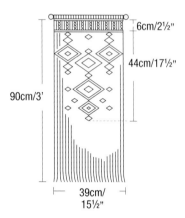

6cm/2½"

44cm/17½"

90cm/3'

39cm/ 15½"

## Hiding Cords

*Hide the other end as a mirror image.

Turn your work over and weave the end of the cord through the second knot using a needle.

Pull the cord so it becomes taut.

Tie a knot at the end of the cord just next to the knot that you weaved the cord through. Cut off any excess cord to hide.

Knotting Diagram ❶

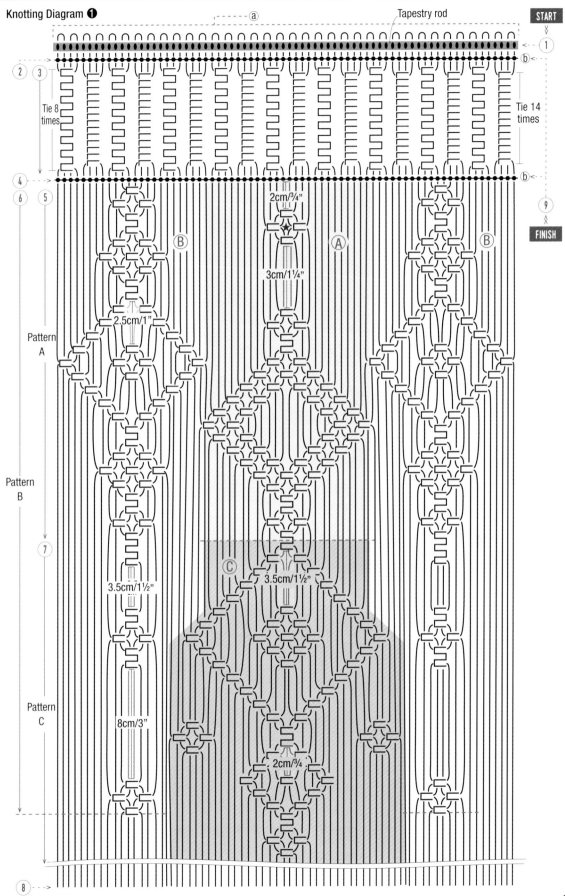

# ITEM J

## V-Pattern Tapestry
### INSTRUCTIONS_P.54

Create a diamond-shape with Clove Hitch
Knots at the center and tie a large Square
Knot inside of the diamond. Contrasting
large and small knots brings out the
playfulness of this particular design.

Design: Aki Hagino

## Materials

Natural-color cotton cord (3mm): Approx.
86m/94yds long

ⓐ Working cord: 300cm/10' long, 28 pieces
ⓑ Filler cord: 40cm/15¾" long, 3 pieces
ⓒ Hanging loop: 1 piece, length as desired
Tapestry rod: 31cm/12¼", 1 piece

## Techniques

Horizontal Clove Hitch (see p.18)
Square Knot (see p.10)
Alternating Square Knots (see p.10)
Diagonal Clove Hitch (see p.14)
Reverse Clove Hitch (see p.14)

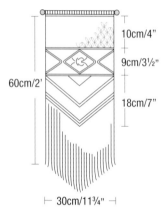

10cm/4"
9cm/3½"
60cm/2'
18cm/7"
30cm/11¾"

1 Fold a piece of cord ⓐ in half and mount it on the tapestry rod. Mount all twenty-eight cords (see p.8 "Basic Mounting Knots").

2 Take a 40cm/15¾" piece of ⓑ (tie an Overhand Knot at the end and pin it down). From the leftmost cord ⓐ, tie one row of Horizontal Clove Hitches using cord ⓑ as the filler.

3 Divide ⓐ into a group of four cords. Move down 1.5cm/⅝" and tie Alternating Square Knots. Make five rows.

4 Move down 1.5cm/⅝" from the last knot tied in step 3. Tie one row of Horizontal Clove Hitches in a manner similar to step 2.

5 Begin to make the top half of Pattern A. Divide ⓐ into four groups of fourteen cords. On each group, tie a row of Square Knots and then a row of Reverse Clove Hitches above the red dotted line in the Knotting Diagram.

6 Use eight cords of ⓐ at the center as filler cords. Use the adjoining four cords on each side of the eight cords to tie one Square Knot (adjust the position so it aligns with the vertices of the diamond shape).

7 Go back to the four groups of fourteen cords we worked on in step 5 and tie knots to make the lower half of Pattern A (similar to step 5). Pick each cord you used in step 6 to tie a Square Knot and tie Reverse Clove Hitches.

8 Repeat step 2.

9 Begin to make Pattern B. First, tie Alternating Square Knots to make the reverse triangle at the center. Next, tie the knots to make the top V-shape pattern (begin tying a Square Knot from the outside. Skip two cords on each knot as you move down diagonally. Lastly, tie one Square Knot at the center). Finally, tie knots to make the bottom V-shaped pattern.

10 Trim the ends of ⓐ to your desired length.

11 Hide the ends of both ⓑ cords you used in steps 2 and 4.

12 Attach a cord ⓒ to the rod with a Gathering Knot to complete.

Knotting Diagram

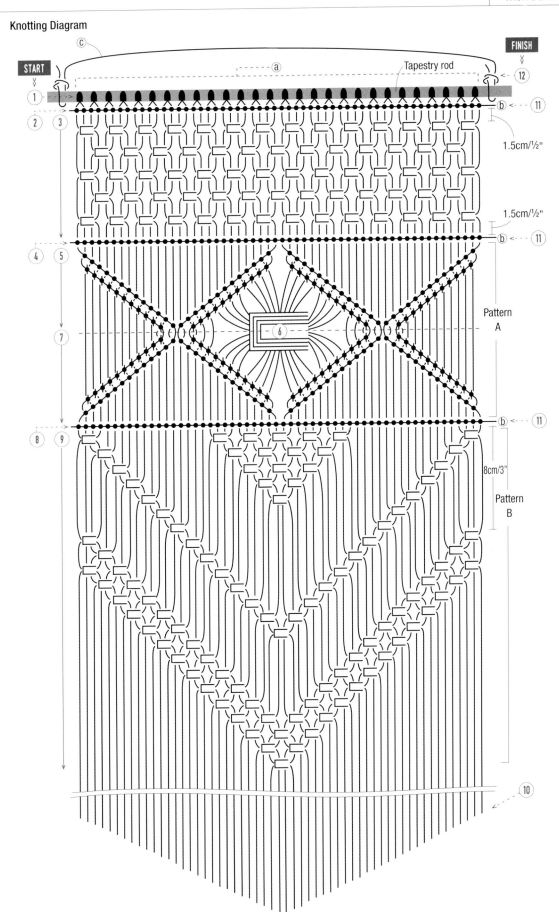

START

FINISH

① ② ③ ④ ⑤ ⑦ ⑧ ⑨ ⑩ ⑪ ⑫

ⓐ ⓑ ⓒ

Tapestry rod

1.5cm/½"

1.5cm/½"

Pattern A

8cm/3"

Pattern B

55

# ITEM K

**Sample Tapestry**
INSTRUCTIONS_P.58

Your sample sennit turns into a tapestry. This tapestry uses seven different knots.

Design: Etsuko Usami

ITEM L

**Dream Catcher**
INSTRUCTIONS_P.60

A dream catcher is a Native American protective charm. It is believed to ward off nightmares and bring good dreams. It makes a great gift for that someone special.

Design: Shoko Hitomi

**Materials**  Natural-color cotton cord: 25.3m/28yds long
Gray: 14.4m/16yds long
Light blue: 8.5m/10yds long
Tapestry rod: 27cm/10⅝", 1 piece

**Techniques**  Square Knot (see p.10) / Alternating Square
Knots (see p.10) / 4-Ply Round Lanyard (see
p.13) / 3-Ply Braids (see p.13) / Spiral Knot (see
p.9) / Alternating Lark's Head Knots (see p.12)
/ Wrapping Knot (see p.15) / Vertical Lark's
Head Knot (see p.12) / Sailor's Knot (see p.15) /
Overhand Knot (see p.15)

**Cord Length**

| Color | Knots | Cord Length | Pieces |
|---|---|---|---|
| Natural ■ | Ⓐ Square Knot | 400cm/13 | 2 pcs |
| | Ⓖ Alternating Square Knots | 270cm/9' | 2 pcs |
| | | 340cm/11' | 2 pcs |
| | Ⓔ 4-Ply Round Lanyard | 150cm/4 | 2 pcs |
| | Ⓒ 3-Ply Braids | 50cm/2' | 1 pcs |
| | Hanging loop | 80cm/31½" | 2 pcs |
| Gray ■ | Ⓑ Spiral Knot | 380cm/12'6" | 2 pcs |
| | Ⓓ Alternating Square Knots + Alternating Lark's Head Knots | 150cm/4 | 4 pcs |
| | Ⓓ Wrapping Knot | 30cm/11¾" | 1 pcs |
| | Ⓒ 3-Ply Braids | 50cm/2' | 1 pcs |
| Light blue ■ | Ⓕ Vertical Lark's Head Knots | 400cm/13 | 2 pcs |
| | Ⓒ 3-Ply Braids | 50cm/2' | 1 pcs |

**1** Refer to Knotting Diagram ❶. Mount two cords of Ⓐ on the left-side of the rod (see "Arrangement" and p.8 "Mounting Knot (Double)"). Tie Square Knots for 55cm/21⅝" using the outermost cord on each side with the inner two cords as the filler cords.

**2** On the right-side of Ⓐ mount two cords of Ⓑ (see "Arrangement"). Tie a Left-Twisted Spiral Knot for 50cm/2' using the outermost cord on each side with the inner two cords as the filler.

**3** On the right-side of Ⓑ mount three cords of Ⓒ (one cord from each color). Tie 3-Ply Braids for 9cm/3½" using the two cords in each ply.

**4** At the end of the 3-Ply Braids, tie a Gathering Knot using two natural-color cords.

**5** On the right-side of the 3-Ply Braids mount four cords of 150cm/4' long Ⓓ after folding them in half. As specified in the Knotting Diagram, tie Alternating Square Knots and Alternating Lark's Head Knots.

**6** At the end of step 5, tie a Wrapping Knot using one piece of 30cm/11¾" long Ⓓ.

**7** On the right-side of the knots made in step 6 mount two cords of Ⓔ after folding them in half. Tie a 4-Ply Round Lanyard for 15cm/6".

**8** On the right-side of the knots made in step 7 mount two cords of Ⓕ after folding them in half. As specified in Knotting Diagram, tie a Vertical Lark's Head Knot for 40cm/15¾".

**9** On the right-side of the knots made in step 8 mount four cords of Ⓖ after folding them in half. As specified in the Knotting Diagram, tie Alternating Square Knots for 45cm/17¾". This concludes the knot making process.

**10-14** Refer to Knotting Diagram ❷. In order of 10 through 14, attach the end of each cord (where specified on the rod) using a Horizontal Clove Hitch. Tie an Overhand Knot on the end of each cord.

**15** Fold the two cords for the hanging loop and attach them to the rod (see p.8 "Basic Mounting Knots").

**16** Make one Overhand Knot using two strands on each side of the hanging loop.

**17** Tie a Sailor's Knot to close the loop to complete.

**Knotting Diagram ❷**

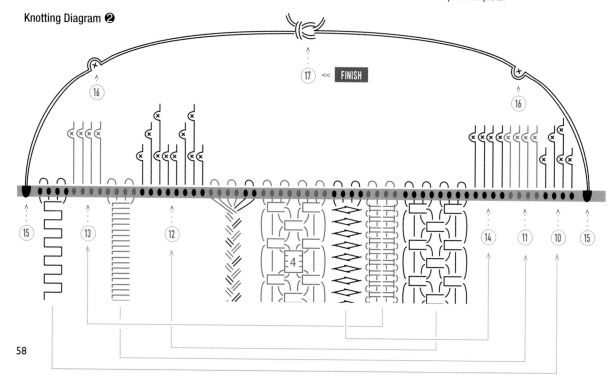

# Knotting Diagram ❶

**START** >>

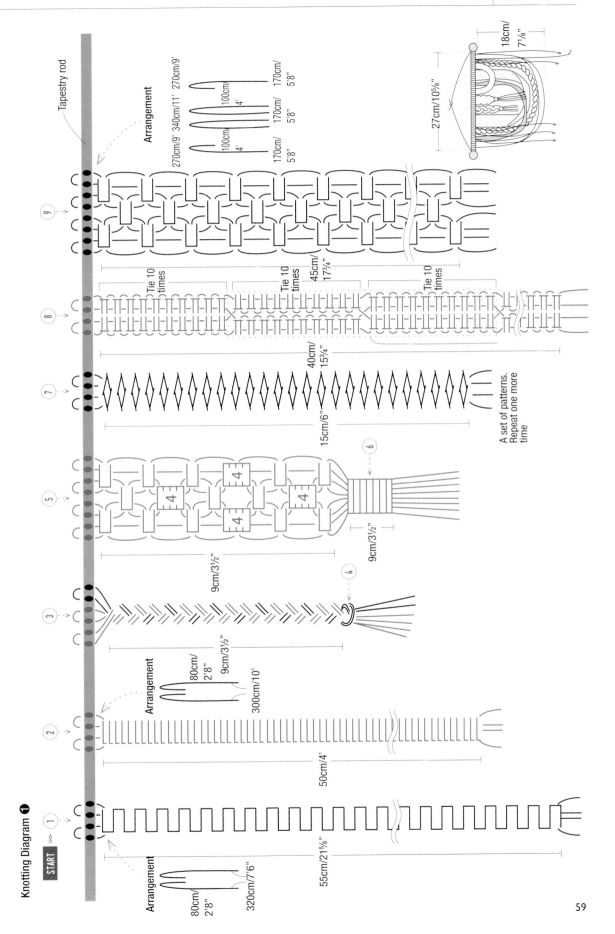

Tapestry rod

**①** →

Arrangement

80cm/
2'8"

320cm/7'6"

55cm/21⁵⁄₈"

**②** →

Arrangement

80cm/
2'8"

9cm/3½"

300cm/10'

50cm/4'

**③** →

9cm/3½"

**④**

9cm/3½"

**⑤** →

4
4
4
4

9cm/3½"

**⑥**

**⑦** →

40cm/
15¾"

15cm/6"

A set of patterns.
Repeat one more
time

**⑧** →

Tie 10
times

Tie 10
times

45cm/
17¾"

Tie 10
times

**⑨** →

Arrangement

270cm/9'  340cm/11'  270cm/9'

100cm/
4'

100cm/
4'

170cm/
5'8"

170cm/
5'8"

170cm/
5'8"

170cm/
5'8"

18cm/
7⅛"

27cm/10⅝"

59

## Materials

White jute cord, extra fine, 22.5m/25yds long
  ⓐ Working cord: 10m/11yds long, 1 piece
  ⓑ For fringe: 100cm/4' long, 11 pieces
  ⓒ For fringe: 50cm/2' long, 2 pieces
  ⓓ Hanging loop: 25cm/10" long, 2 pieces

Crystal pebbles: 9 pieces

Natural wood beads
  Ⓐ White round 6mm/¼": 26 pieces
  Ⓑ Gray round 6mm/¼": 8 pieces
  Ⓒ Red round 12mm/½": 12 pieces
  Ⓓ Red tube 36mm/1⅜": 5 pieces
  Ⓔ Gray tube 14mm/½": 10 pieces
  Ⓕ Red disk 10mm/⅜": 30 pieces
  Ⓖ Red disk 15mm/⅝": 9 pieces

Feathers: 5 pieces

Metal ring: 23cm/9" diameter, 1 piece

## Techniques

Overhand Knot (see p.15)
Left-Facing Half Hitch (see p.11)

1 Refer to "Starting Knots" and wrap cord ⓐ around the metal ring.

2 Move 6cm/2½" in a clockwise direction from where you started to wrap the metal ring with cord ⓐ, then tie one Left-Facing Half Hitch.

3 Move 7cm/2¾" from the knot you made in step 2 in a clockwise direction. Then, tie one Left-Facing Half Hitch.

4 Repeat step 3 until you tie a knot around the metal ring. Tighten the cord and tie each knot.

5 Begin the second round. Tie one Left-Facing Half Hitch between the knot you made in the previous step. Thread a crystal pebble after making the knot.

6 Begin the third round. Tie one Left-Facing Half Hitch between the knots made in the previous step. Repeat Left-Facing Half Hitches until the space at the center is a 1cm/⅜" diameter circle. Refer to "Hiding Cords at the Center" to hide cords.

7 Twine two cords of ⓓ (refer to "How to Twine Cords") and attach to the metal ring as shown in "How to Attach a Hanging Loop."

8 Fold cords ⓑ and ⓒ in half and attach them to the specified areas as you refer to the Knotting Diagram (see p.8 "Basic Mounting Knots").

9 Twine two cords of ⓑ. As specified in the Knotting Diagram, thread a bead through the twined ⓑ cord and tie one Overhand Knot after threading each bead. This will secure the bead in place. Then, move down 5cm/2" and tie one Overhand Knot. Add quills to a bead and glue them together as desired. Undo the twine at the end of the cord.

10 As for cord ⓒ, as specified in the Knotting Diagram, thread beads and glue a feather on the last bead. Tie an Overhand Knot with two strands to secure the beads in place. Trim off the end of the cord leaving 1cm/⅜" from the Overhand Knot.

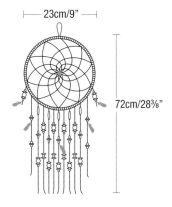

├─ 23cm/9" ─┤

72cm/28⅜"

## How to Twine Cords

Twine each cord in a counter-clockwise direction. → Twist two cords against each other clockwise.

## How to Attach a Hanging Loop

Twine each cord in a clockwise direction.

Metal ring

Basic Mounting Knots (see p.8)

→ Tie an Overhand Knot with the two strands.

## Hide Cords at the Center

④Pass over and under the cord on the opposing side.

The final Left-Facing Half Hitc[h]

⑤Thread the bead.

⑥Pour glue into the hole of the bead. After the glue has dried, trim off any excess cord.

bead ⓒ

①Thread bead ⓒ.

③Thread the bead.

②Pass over and under the cord on the opposing side.

Knotting Diagram

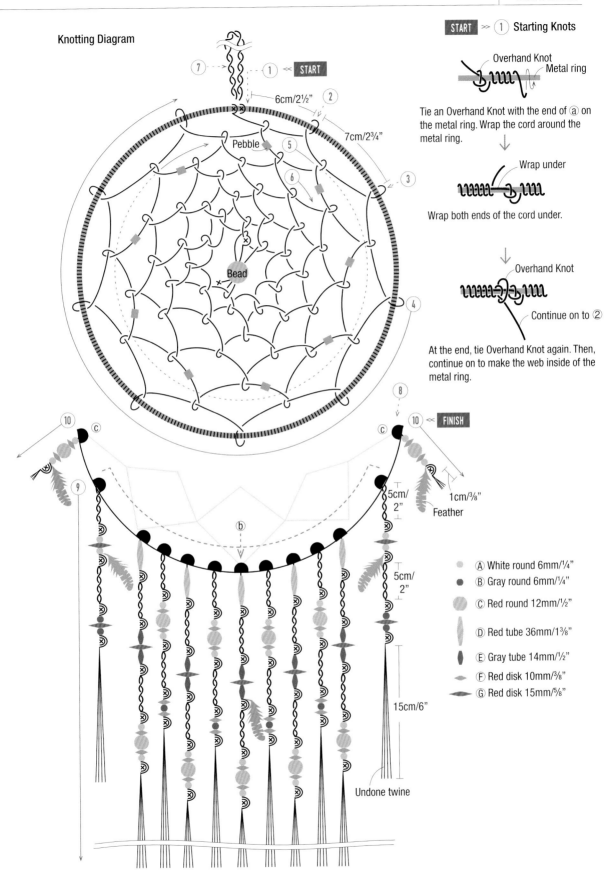

Overhand Knot
Metal ring

Tie an Overhand Knot with the end of ⓐ on the metal ring. Wrap the cord around the metal ring.

Wrap under

Wrap both ends of the cord under.

Overhand Knot

Continue on to ②

At the end, tie Overhand Knot again. Then, continue on to make the web inside of the metal ring.

6cm/2½"

7cm/2¾"

Pebble

Bead

1cm/⅜"
Feather

5cm/2"

5cm/2"

15cm/6"

Undone twine

ⓐ White round 6mm/¼"
ⓑ Gray round 6mm/¼"
ⓒ Red round 12mm/½"
ⓓ Red tube 36mm/1⅜"
ⓔ Gray tube 14mm/½"
ⓕ Red disk 10mm/⅜"
ⓖ Red disk 15mm/⅝"

**FINISH**

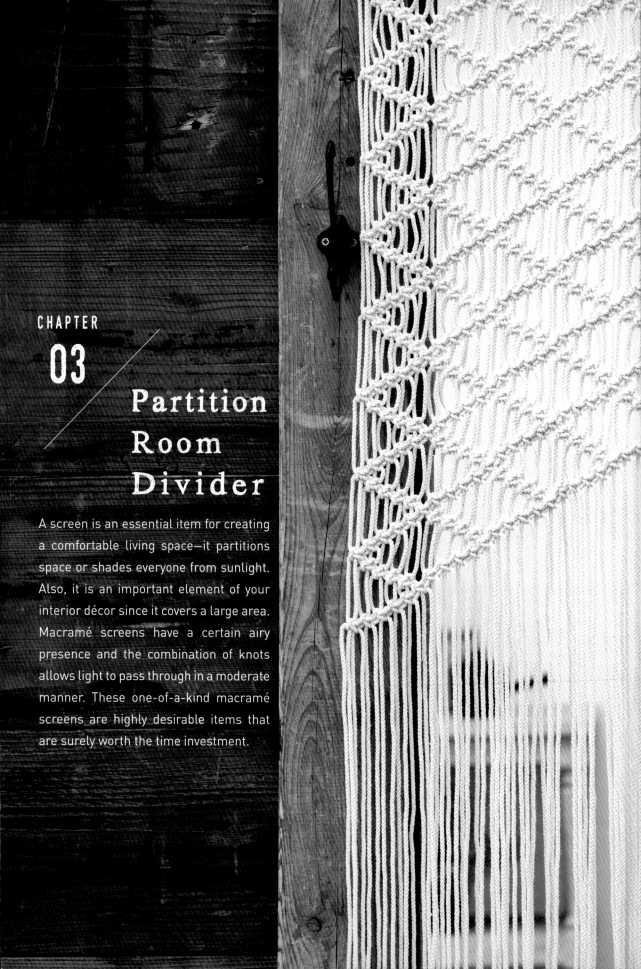

# Partition Room Divider

A screen is an essential item for creating a comfortable living space—it partitions space or shades everyone from sunlight. Also, it is an important element of your interior décor since it covers a large area. Macramé screens have a certain airy presence and the combination of knots allows light to pass through in a moderate manner. These one-of-a-kind macramé screens are highly desirable items that are surely worth the time investment.

ITEM **M**

**Separation Screen**
INSTRUCTIONS_P.60

This screen is made up of 8cm/2⅛"
wide sennit. The sennit is easy to
make because of its narrow width.
Conveniently, you can adjust the
number of sennit on the rod to fit
your chosen space.
Design: Yuko Tsukahara

## Materials

Natural-color cotton cord
(3mm): 360m/394yds long
ⓐ Sennit Ⓐ 380cm/12'6"
long, 2 sets of 10 pieces
ⓑ Sennit Ⓑ: 420m/460yds
long, 2 sets of 10pieces
ⓒ Sennit Ⓐ': 480cm/16'
long, 2 sets of 10 pieces
ⓓ Sennit Ⓑ': 520m/569yds
long, 2 sets of 10 pieces
Tapestry rod: 90cm/3', 1 piece

## Techniques

Square Knot (see p.10) /
Knotted-Loop Button (see
p.12) / Alternating Square
Knots (see p.10)

### Arrangement of the Cords on ①

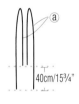

40cm/15¾"

*①-㉔ in the Knotting Diagram indicates
the number of the row for Pattern A (24
rows make one pattern).

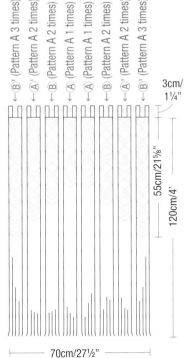

Ⓑ' (Pattern A 3 times)
Ⓐ' (Pattern A 2 times)
Ⓑ (Pattern A 2 times)
Ⓐ (Pattern A 1 times)
Ⓐ (Pattern A 1 times)
Ⓑ (Pattern A 2 times)
Ⓐ' (Pattern A 2 times)
Ⓑ' (Pattern A 3 times)

3cm/1¼"
55cm/21⅝"
120cm/4'
70cm/27½"

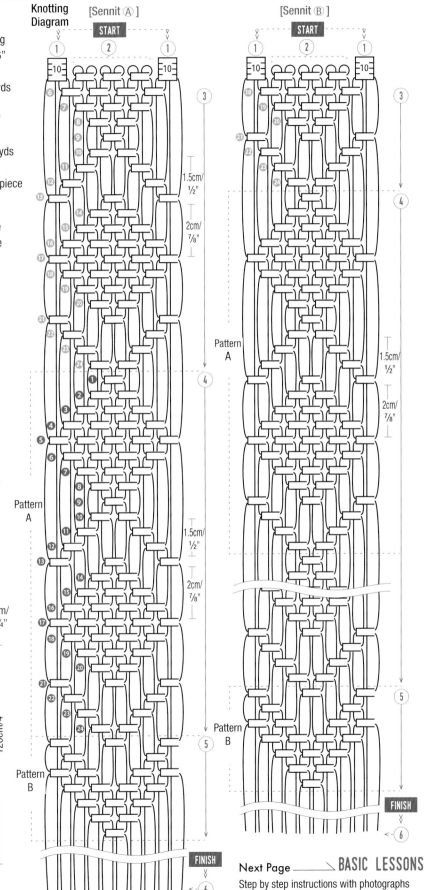

Knotting Diagram

[Sennit Ⓐ]  START

Pattern A

1.5cm/½"

2cm/⅞"

Pattern A

1.5cm/½"

2cm/⅞"

Pattern B

FINISH

[Sennit Ⓑ]  START

Pattern A

1.5cm/½"

2cm/⅞"

Pattern B

FINISH

Next Page ⟶ BASIC LESSONS
Step by step instructions with photographs

# BASIC LESSONS: Separation Screen

The foundation of this screen is a sennit, about 8cm/2⅛" wide, made by tying knots using ten cords. Sennits Ⓐ and Ⓑ are different but they share Pattern A and Pattern B. This section demonstrates steps for making Sennit Ⓐ, which is the foundation sennit for this screen. Also, points out what you need to do differently when you make the Sennits Ⓐ', Ⓑ, and Ⓑ'.

← Watch the tutorial video!
http://www.marchen-art.co.jp/movie/macrame_interior_03

**1-❶** Make a loop for attaching the sennit to a rod. Take two cords of ⓐ. Fold the cords at 40cm/15¾" down from the center and lay them down with placing the short end on the inside (when you make other sennits, use this same placement).

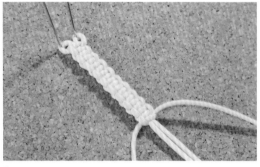

**1-❷** The inner two cords are the filler cords. Tie ten Square Knots with the outer two cords.

**1-❸** Thread the filler cords through the initial loops of the sennit to create a loop with the Square Knot sennit.

**1-❹** Tie one Square Knot at the base of the loop. This concludes the Knotted-Loop Button. Make another Knotted-Loop Button.

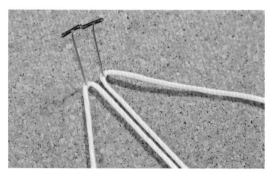

**2-❶** Take two cords of ⓐ. Fold each cord in half and lay them side by side as above (lay the cords same way for ⓑ-ⓓ).

**2-❷** The inner two cords are filler cords. Tie one Square Knot using the outer two cords. Make two more sets like this.

**3-❶** Lay three of the simple Square Knots side by side. Then, lay each Knotted-Loop Button section outside the three simple Square Knots.

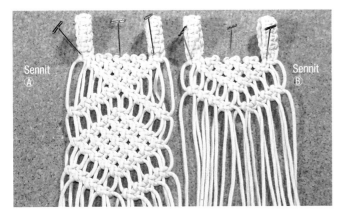

## 3 -❷

Refer to the Knotting Diagram. Tie rows 6 through 24 of Pattern A. (Do the same for Sennit Ⓐ'. For Sennit Ⓑ and Ⓑ', tie rows 18 through 24 of Pattern A.)

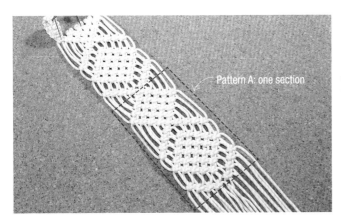

Pattern A: one section

## 4

Continue to make a set of Pattern A (for Sennit Ⓐ' and Ⓑ, make two sets of Pattern A. For sennit Ⓑ', make three sets of Pattern A).

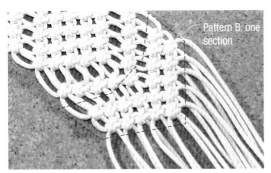

Pattern B: one section

**5** Lastly, tie the knots to make "Pattern B."

Finishing Up

Sennit Ⓑ' Sennit Ⓐ' Sennit Ⓑ' Sennit Ⓐ Sennit Ⓐ Sennit Ⓑ Sennit Ⓐ' Sennit Ⓑ'

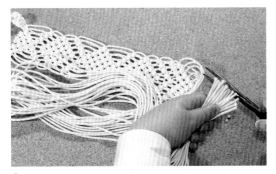

**6** Excluding the loop portion, measure 120cm/4' from the top edge of the sennit and trim off any excess to complete.

Make two sets of each sennit Ⓐ, Ⓐ', Ⓑ, and Ⓑ'. Place on the rod in the order of Ⓑ'→Ⓐ'→Ⓑ→Ⓐ→Ⓐ→Ⓑ→Ⓐ'→Ⓑ' to complete.

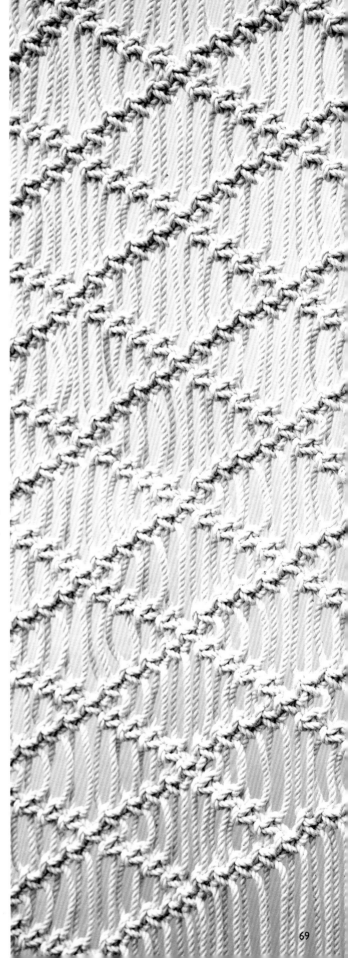

## Diamond-Shaped Pattern Curtain
### INSTRUCTIONS_P.70

The interconnected knots in this curtain make a diamond-shape. This curtain, separated into three sections, can be used as a room partition.

Design: Sawa Matsuda

**Materials**
Natural-color cotton cord: 668m/731yds long
ⓐ Left/right section: 650cm/21' 6" long, 64 pieces
ⓑ Center section: 600cm/20' long, 42 pieces
Curtain rod: 120cm/4', 1 piece

**Techniques**
Alternating Half Hitch (see p.11)
Square Knot (see p.10)
Alternating Square Knots (see p.10)

*[ ] indicates the left and right section
*<> indicates the center section

1 Refer to "Starting Knots" for the loops. Use two cords from [ⓐ] and <ⓑ>.

2 As specified in the Knotting Diagram, tie Alternating Square Knots until row 5 with the loop you made in step 1 while adding a new cord ([ⓐ] <ⓑ>), folded in half, to each row on both the left and right side. This makes a loop with an inverted V-pattern piece. For the piece on the left-edge add a new cord ([ⓐ] <ⓑ>), folded in half, to each row on the right side (this will make the right half of the inverted V-pattern). For the piece on the right-edge add a new cord ([ⓐ] <ⓑ>), folded in half, to each row on the left side (this will make the left half of the inverted V-pattern).

3 Repeat steps 1 and 2 to make the necessary components for the left, center, and right sections. For each left and right section, you will need two pieces of loop with an inverted V-pattern, a left-edge piece, and a right-edge piece. For the center section, three pieces of loop with an inverted V-pattern, a left-edge piece, and a right-edge piece (see Size Chart).

4 Arrange the edge pieces, the loops with an inverted V-pattern [2 pcs] <3 pcs>, from left to right. Secure them on the board and tie Alternating Square Knots on row 6 (so each piece will be connected). Section width: [30cm/11¾"] <40cm/15¾">.

5 As specified in the Knotting Diagram, tie row 7 through 11 (the Alternating Square Knot diamond is complete now).

6 Continue to work on making diamond-shaped outlines as specified in the Knotting Diagram with Alternating Square Knots. Tie knots from [row 25] and <row 15> so the line slants down to the right to [row 30], <row 18> (for the left section slant down to the left).

7 Trim off the ends of the cords to make the curtain 180cm/6' long.

8 Loop the rod through all sections to complete.

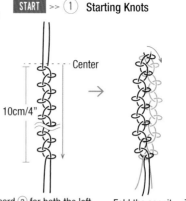

START >> ① **Starting Knots**

Center

10cm/4"

Use cord ⓐ for both the left and right sections. Use cord ⓑ for the center section. Tie Alternating Half Hitches for 10cm/4" from the center of the cord.

Fold the sennit in half.

The two cords at the forefront are the filler cords. Tie one Square Knot using the two cords at the backside. (This Square Knot is row 1 of the Alternating Square Knots).

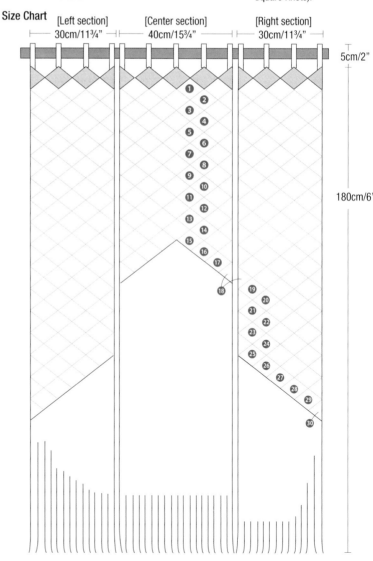

**Size Chart**
[Left section] 30cm/11¾"  [Center section] 40cm/15¾"  [Right section] 30cm/11¾"

5cm/2"

180cm/6'

◇ Diamond-pattern with Alternating Square Knots ❶ - ❸⓪

◇ Diamond-shaped outline

Row# to tie diamond-shaped outline

**Knotting Diagram** (Right section. Add one piece in step 3 for the center section. See Size Chart for making diamond-shaped outlines for the center and left section.)

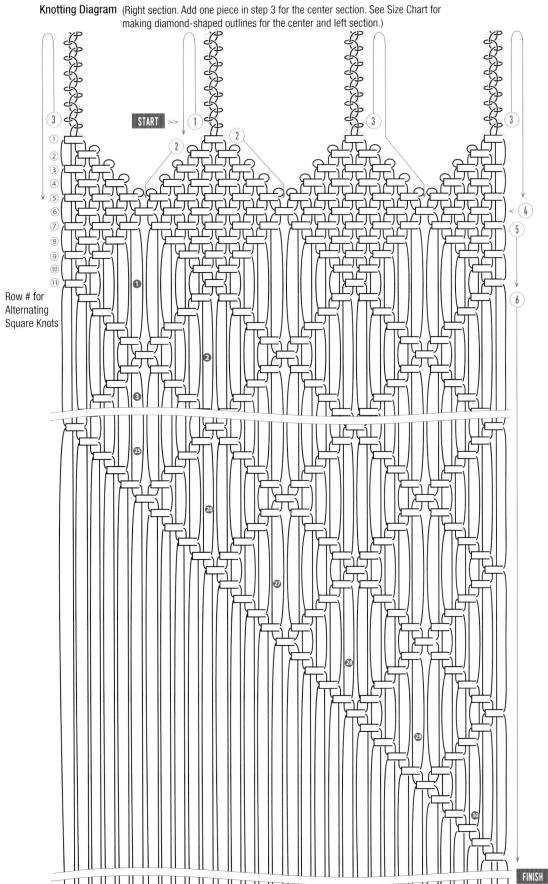

Row # for
Alternating
Square Knots

## ITEM 0

### Single Curtain
#### INSTRUCTIONS_P.74

This curtain is made for a waist-height window. The eye pleasing lace-like design is created with a combination of various types of knots that gently block the sunlight.

Design: Michiko Nakamura

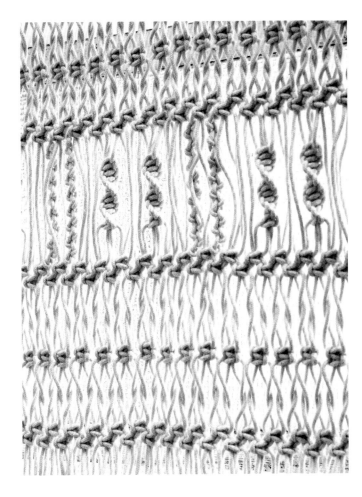

**Materials**

Natural-color cotton cord (2mm):
268.8m/294yds long
ⓐ: 340cm/11'2" long, 24 pieces
ⓑ: 320cm/10'6" long, 36 pieces
ⓒ: 300cm/10' long, 24 pieces
Tapestry rod: 60cm/2', 1 piece

**Techniques**

Spiral Knot (see p.10)
Alternating Half Hitch (see p.11)
Alternating Square Knots (see p.10)
Spiral Knot (see p.9)
Overhand Knot (see p.15)

1 Fold cords ⓐ-ⓑ in half. As shown in the Knotting Diagram, lay out each cord horizontally and secure using a pin. Tie one Square Knot with a group of four cords. For ⓐ move down 3cm/1" from the center, then tie one Square Knot (now you have a loop to mount for the rod).

2 Tie two rows of Alternating Square Knots without moving down a row.

3 Tie the knots to make Pattern A as specified in the Knotting Diagram. When you move down a row, pin down the cord where you move down to make the knot uniform.

4 As specified in Knotting Diagram, tie knots to make Pattern B (arrange the Alternating Square Knots). Move down 3cm/1¼" after working each row, then cross the filler and working cords twice before tying Alternating Square Knots.

5 As specified in the Knotting Diagram, tie knots to make Pattern C (a combination of Alternating Half Hitches and Spiral Knots). Leave a 1.5cm/⅝" space before and after the Spiral Knots.

*Continue on to Knotting Diagram❷ on pgs. 76 through 77.

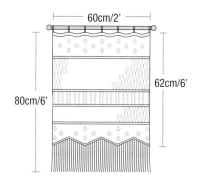

**Knotting Pattern ❶**

Third repetition of the Pattern

3cm/1¼"
2cm/⅞" — Cross
2cm/⅞"
Tie 1.5 Square Knots
2cm/⅞"
12cm/4¾"
2cm/⅞"
3cm/1¼"
3cm/1¼"
18cm/7"
3cm/1¼"
3cm/1¼"
12cm/4¾"

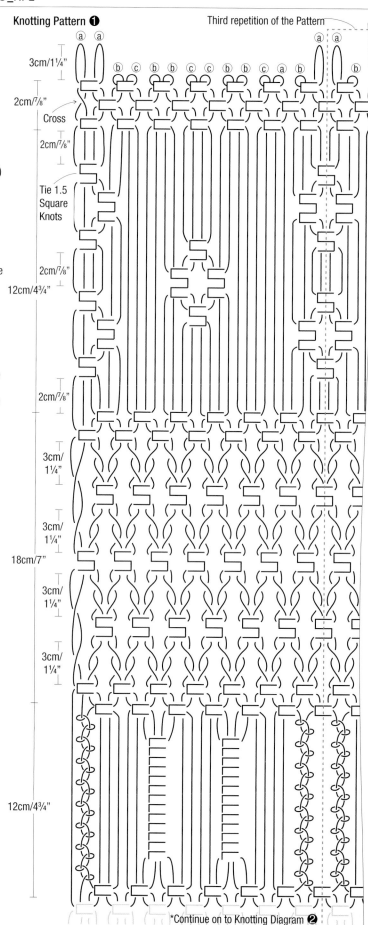

60cm/2'
62cm/6'
80cm/6'

*Continue on to Knotting Diagram ❷

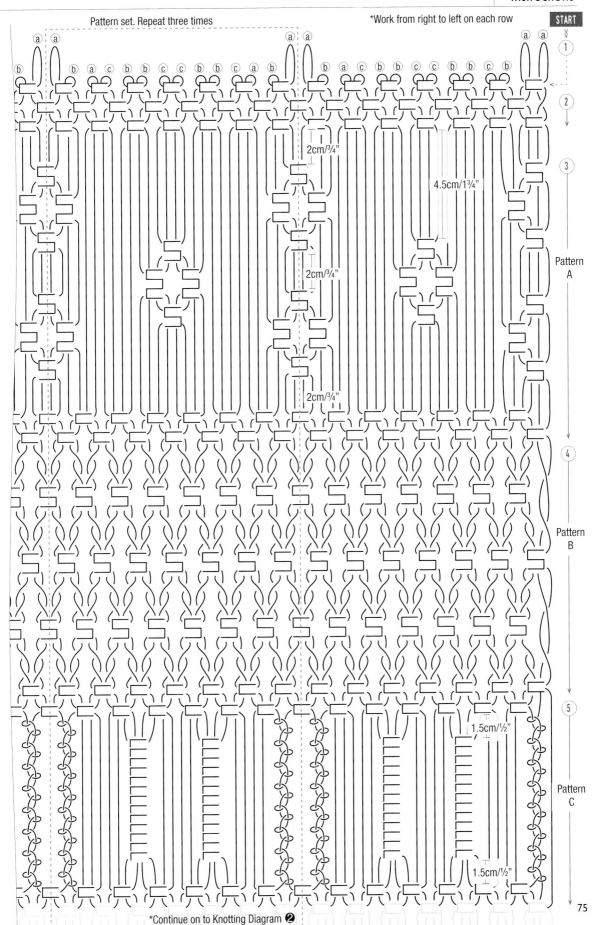

Pattern set. Repeat three times

*Work from right to left on each row

START

1

2

3

2cm/³⁄₄"

4.5cm/1³⁄₄"

Pattern A

2cm/³⁄₄"

2cm/³⁄₄"

4

Pattern B

5

1.5cm/¹⁄₂"

Pattern C

1.5cm/¹⁄₂"

*Continue on to Knotting Diagram ❷

*Continued from Knotting Diagram ❶ on pgs. 74 through 75.

**6** As specified in the Knotting Diagram, make Pattern D. The method for tying the knots is the same as Pattern B in step 4, but move down 4cm/1½" after working on each row.

**7** As specified in the Knotting Diagram, tie knots to make Pattern E (pay attention because the pattern segments change here). As you continue to work, tie Overhand Knots with two cords as desired. Work in both directions for the knots marked with a ★. Shift two cords, then tie one Square Knot without skipping a cord so the knots line up like a mountain.

**8** Trim off the cord ends so the curtain is 80cm/31½" long. Then, feed the rod through the curtain to complete.

### Knotting Pattern ❷

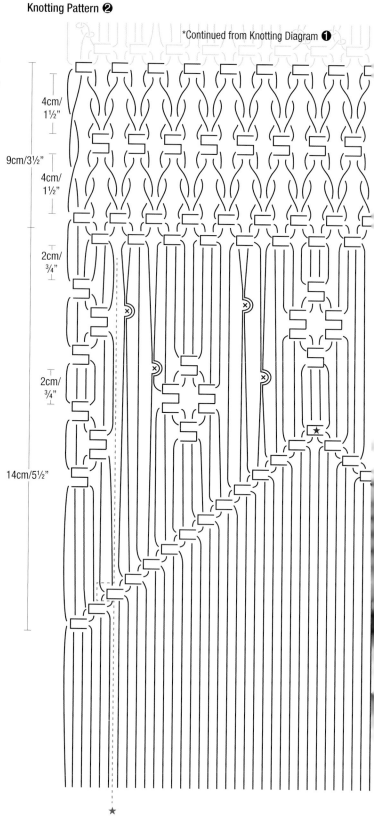

*Continued from Knotting Diagram ❶

4cm/1½"

9cm/3½"

4cm/1½"

2cm/¾"

2cm/¾"

14cm/5½"

★

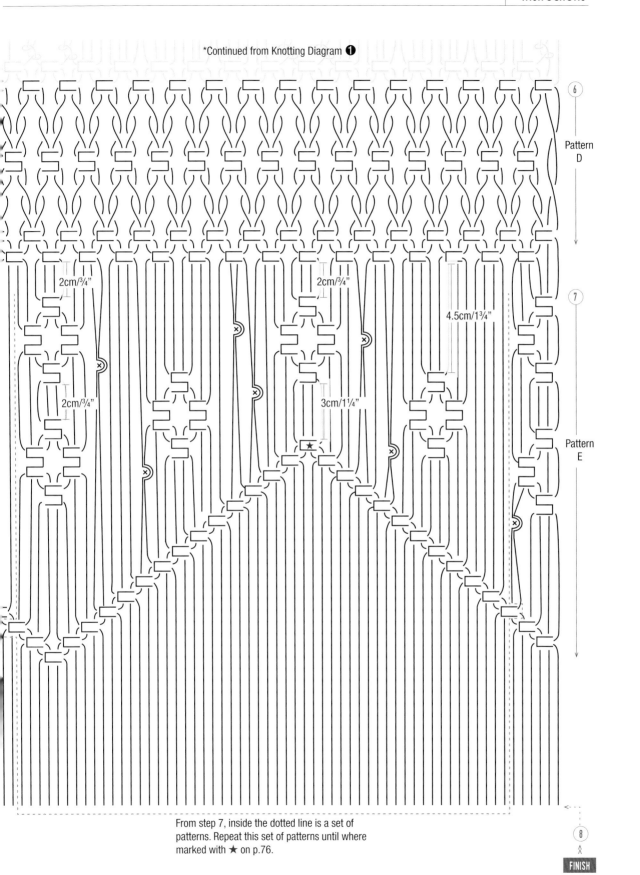

*Continued from Knotting Diagram ❶

6

Pattern
D

2cm/³⁄₄"

2cm/³⁄₄"

7

4.5cm/1³⁄₄"

2cm/³⁄₄"

3cm/1¹⁄₄"

★

Pattern
E

From step 7, inside the dotted line is a set of
patterns. Repeat this set of patterns until where
marked with ★ on p.76.

8

FINISH

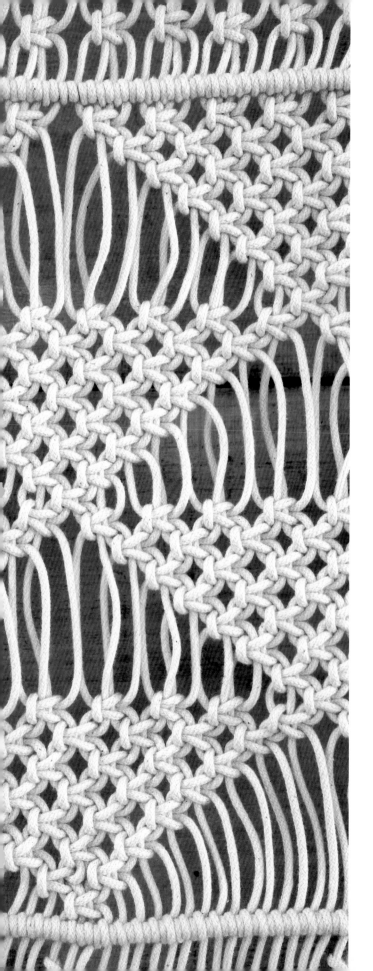

ITEM **P**

## Triangle-Shaped Pattern Screen
### INSTRUCTIONS_P.80

This modern pattern arranges reversed
triangular shapes made with Alternating
Square Knots. Just hanging this tapestry
drastically changes the impression of
a room.

Design: Aki Hagino

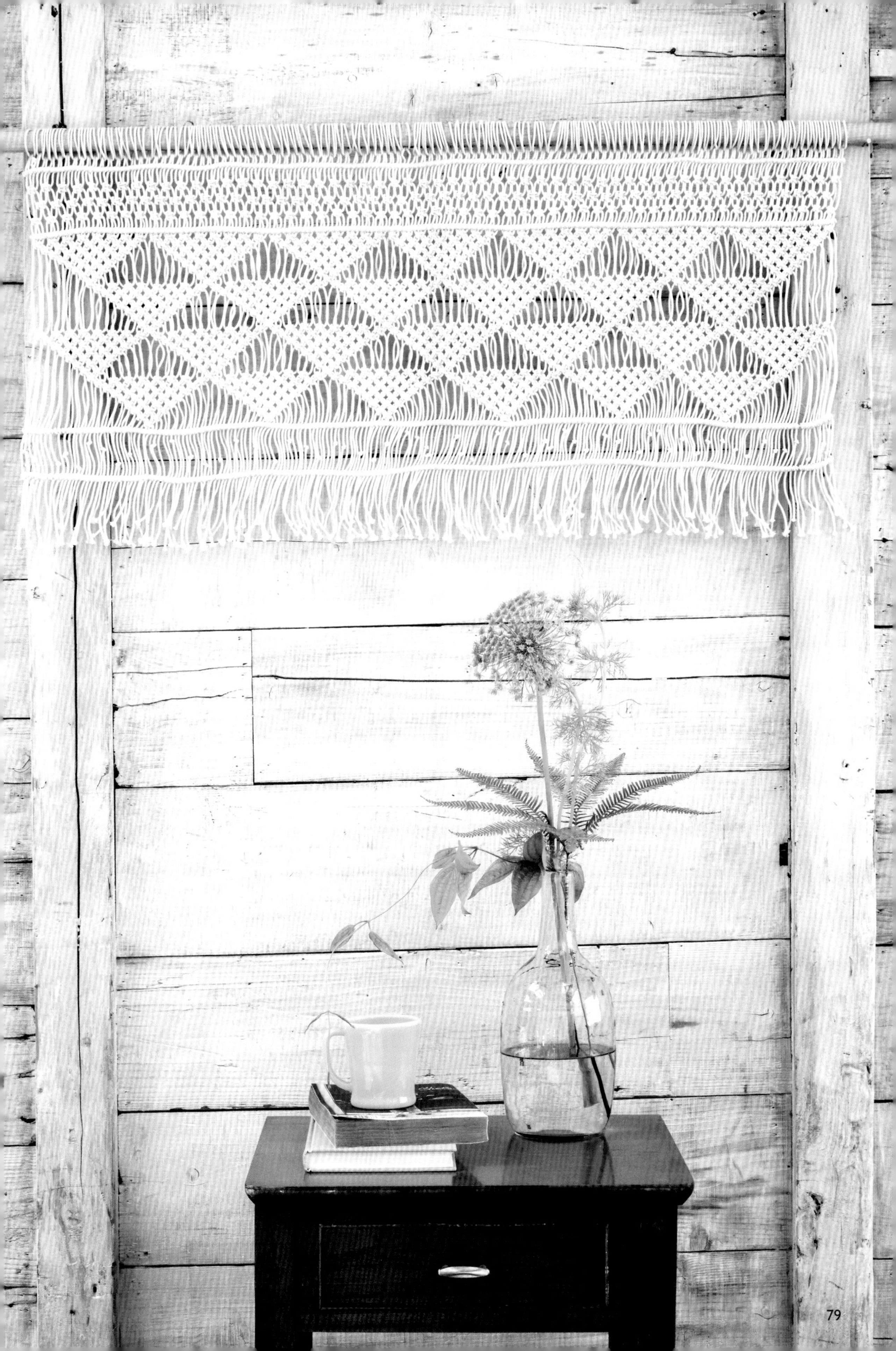

**Materials**

Natural-color cotton cord (2mm):
Approx. 276m/302yds long
ⓐ Working cord: 240cm/8' long, 112 pieces
ⓑ Filler cord: 140cm/4'6" long, 4 pieces
ⓒ Hanging loop: Your desired length,
    1 piece
Wood rod: 120cm/4', 1 piece

**Techniques**

Square Knot (see p.10)
Alternating Square Knots (see p.10)
Horizontal Clove Hitch (see p.8)

1 Hang the wood rod on the hooks. Mount all cord ⓐ, folded in half, on the rod (see p.8, "Basic Mounting Knots").

2 From rightmost cord ⓐ tie one Horizontal Clove Hitch, using ⓑ as the filler. Work on subsequent cords of ⓐ to make a row of Horizontal Clove Hitches.

3 Take four cords from the rightmost strands. Move down 2.5cm/1" and tie one Square Knot using the inner two cords as filler.

4 Move down 2.5cm/1" and tie Alternating Square Knots for two rows.

5 Move down 2.5cm/1" from the second row of Alternating Square Knots, repeat step 2.

6 As specified in the Knotting Diagram, tie Alternating Square Knots to make four reverse triangular shaped patterns. Tie Alternating Square Knots without skipping any cords. Pay attention because the right and left sides have different repetitive elements.

7 From the rightmost cord of ⓐ, tie one Horizontal Clove Hitch using ⓑ as the filler cord. Work on subsequent pieces of ⓐ to make a row of Horizontal Clove Hitches just below the final Square Knot of the last reverse triangular shaped pattern.

8 Tie Overhand Knots with each piece of ⓐ at random, but within 4cm/1½" from the row made in step 7.

9 Move down 4cm/1½" from the row made in step 7. Tie a row of Horizontal Clove Hitches using ⓑ.

10 Trim the ends of cords to the desired length.

11 Dispose of cord ⓑ ends at the back of your work (see p.17) to complete.

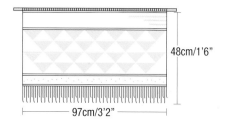

48cm/1'6"

97cm/3'2"

**Knotting Diagram**

Wood rod

Sixth pattern

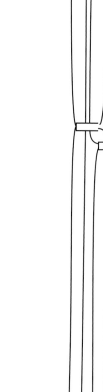

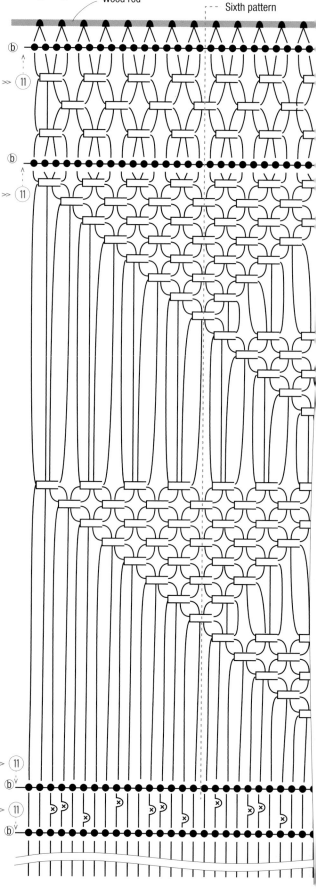

FINISH >> 11

ⓑ

FINISH >> 11

ⓑ

FINISH >> 11

ⓑ

FINISH >> 11

ⓑ

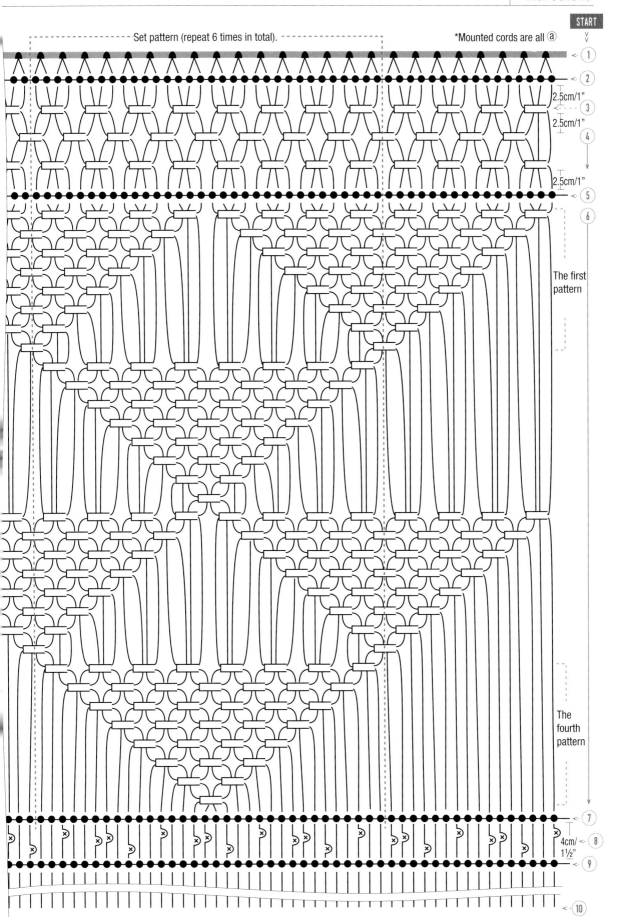

START

*Mounted cords are all ⓐ

Set pattern (repeat 6 times in total).

1

2

2.5cm/1"

3

2.5cm/1"

4

2.5cm/1"

5

6

The first pattern

The fourth pattern

7

8

4cm/1½"

9

10

CHAPTER

## 04

# Accessories

Unique everyday items and accessories are quite effective to set the tone for your interior décor. These items are compact, but they work wonders when accentuating your chosen space. You can easily make use of any one of these small items for your project. Why not give accessory macramé a try?

## ITEM Q

### Net Bag
**INSTRUCTIONS_P.86**

This net bag is perfect for storing fruits and vegetables because of its superior airflow. Kitchens, which tend to be dominated by natural colors, can really benefit from vibrantly colored cords.

Design: Märchen Art Studio

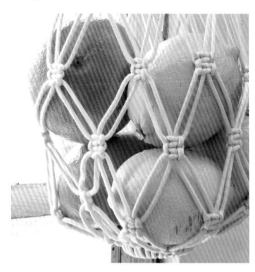

## ITEM R

### Bottle Cover
**INSTRUCTIONS_P.88**

An ordinary empty bottle can be turned into a veritable *objet d'art* just by covering it with macramé work. The bottle cover is considered a standard macramé work.

Design: tama5

**Materials**  Yellow cotton cord (3mm): 41m/45yds long
ⓐ Working cord: 250cm/8'2" long, 16 pieces
ⓑ For Wrapping Knots: 100cm/4' long, 1 piece
Wooden ring: 44mm/1¾" diameter, 1 piece

**Techniques**  Square Knot (see p.10)
Alternating Square Knots (see p.10)
Wrapping Knot (see p.15)
Overhand Knot (see p.15)

1 Fold one piece of cord ⓐ in half and mount to the wooden ring. Mount all sixteen cords of ⓐ (see p.8, "Basic Mounting Knots").

2 Divide ⓐ into a group of four cords. Tie two Square Knots on each group.

3 Move down 3cm/1¼" and tie one row of Alternating Square Knots (tie two Square Knots on each knot).

4 Move down 4cm/1½" and tie two rows of Alternating Square Knots (tie two Square Knots on each knot).

5 Move down 5cm/2" and tie three rows of Alternating Square Knots (tie two Square Knots on each knot).

6 Take half of the cords (sixteen) and tie one Square Knot using the outermost two cords on each side—meaning that the inner twelve cords would be the filler cords (move down 10cm/4" from the last knot in step 5).

7 Divide the sixteen cords that you worked in step 6 into one group of six cords and two groups of five cords. Then, tie 3-Ply Braids for 15cm/6".

8 Repeat steps 6 through 7 with the remaining sixteen cords.

9 Pile the ends of the 3-Ply Braids on top of each other, then tie a Wrapping Knot using cord ⓑ to secure the ends together.

10 Move down 10cm/4" from the end of the Wrapping Knot. Tie an Overhand Knot on each cord to complete.

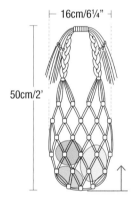

├─ 16cm/6¼" ─┤

50cm/2'

**Knotting Diagram ❶: The second row from the mounting knots**

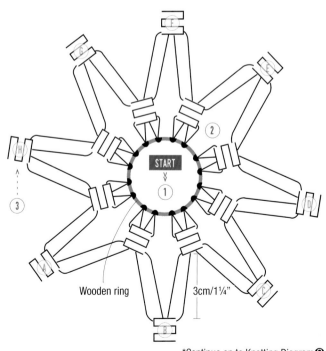

START

Wooden ring          3cm/1¼"

*Continue on to Knotting Diagram ❷

Knotting Diagram ❷: From the third row on

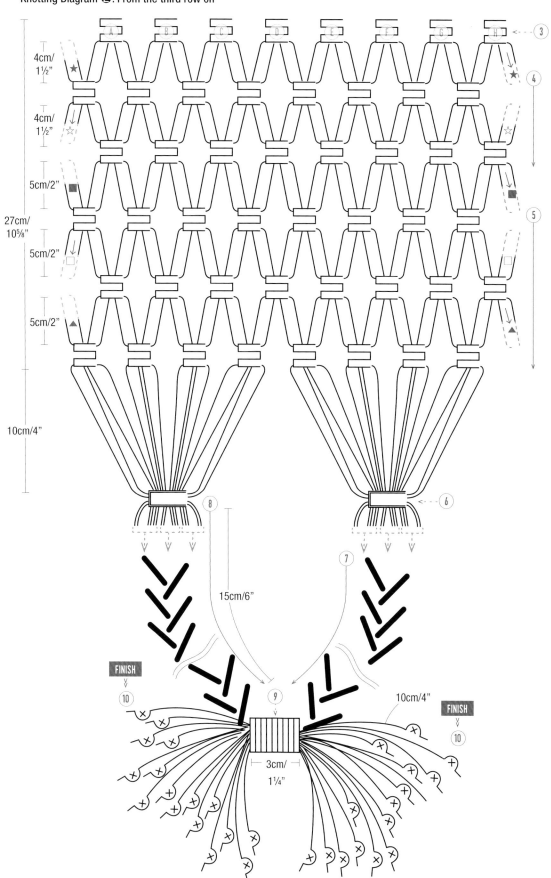

4cm/
1½"

4cm/
1½"

5cm/2"

27cm/
10⅝"

5cm/2"

5cm/2"

10cm/4"

15cm/6"

FINISH

10cm/4"

FINISH

3cm/
1¼"

## Materials

Hemp fine cord: 14 pieces 150cm/4' long
*ⓐ: White, ⓑ: Natural-color
*Bottle size: Inner diameter of opening 2.5cm/1",
bottom diameter 4.8cm/2",
height 19cm/7½"

## Techniques

Square Knot (see p.10)
Alternating Square Knots (see p.10)

NOTES Bottle Cover

• Tie each knot uniformly, while following the shape of the bottle, in order to create a beautiful bottle cover. Stretch both the filler and working cords and tie a Square Knot at the center of the four filler cords to create Alternating Square Knots. Be sure not to stretch the cords too tight, but also don't leave them too loose. Repeating these actions forms beautiful Alternating Square Knots along the shape of the bottle.

• Feel free to adjust the number of knots according to the size of you bottle. If your bottle's mouth is wider than the bottle used here, adjust the space between the cords you mount in step 1. Also, calculate the approximate length required for your bottle using the following formula—[(bottle height + bottom radius) x 7].

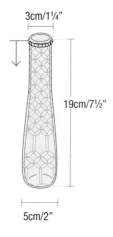

3cm/1¼"

19cm/7½"

5cm/2"

*Tie knots uniformly, while pulling the cords taut, so that the spacing of the Alternating Square Knots accords with the shape of the bottle (i.e. the size of the bottle dictates the spacing).

1 On a piece of hemp cord—a holding cord—mount the other thirteen cords by folding them in half (see p.8 "Mounting Knot (Double)").

2 Wrap the holding cord around the mouth of the bottle. Both ends of the holding cord are the filler cords now. Take one cord from the left and right side of the filler cords and tie a Square Knot two times. Stretch the filler cords firmly so the cords run along the bottle.

3 Starting from the Square Knots in step 2, divide the cords into groups of four cords and tie Square Knots twice on each group.

4 Tie eleven rows of Alternating Square Knots (two per knot).

5 For the next row, tie Square Knots ten times on each group.

6 Tie two rows of Alternating Square Knots (two per knot).

7 Repeat steps 5 through 6. When you reach the bottom of the bottle, tie the knots tightly so your bottle cover fits snugly.

8 For the next row, tie five Square Knots on each group.

9 Tie a row of Alternating Square Knots (two per knot). Tie the knots tightly towards the bottom center.

10 Tie a row of Alternating Square Knots (one per knot). After making the final knot, trim the cord ends short and glue to secure. Complete.

Knotting Diagram

START

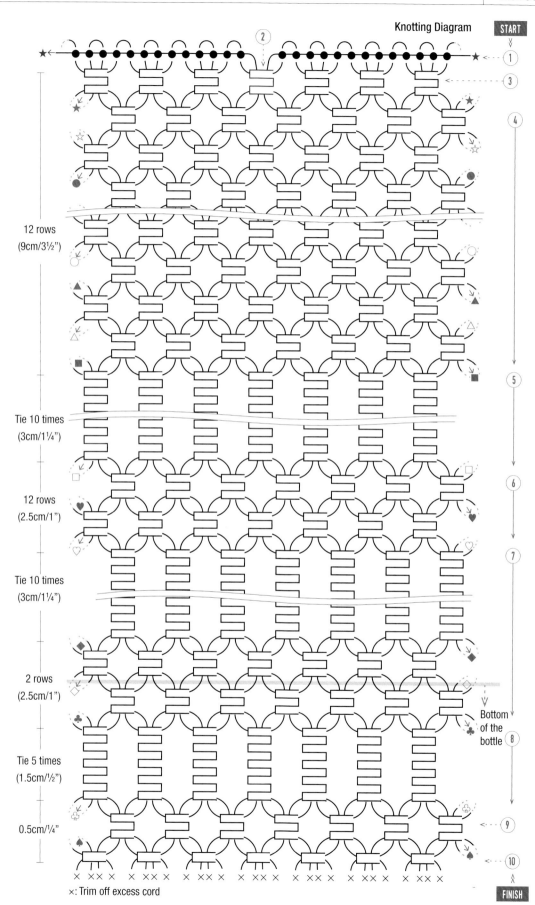

①

②

③

④

12 rows
(9cm/3½")

⑤

Tie 10 times
(3cm/1¼")

⑥

12 rows
(2.5cm/1")

⑦

Tie 10 times
(3cm/1¼")

2 rows
(2.5cm/1")

Bottom
of the
bottle ⑧

Tie 5 times
(1.5cm/½")

⑨

0.5cm/¼"

⑩

×: Trim off excess cord

FINISH

## ITEM S

### Kettle Mat
**INSTRUCTIONS_P.92**

This ethnic-feeling, doughnut-shaped kettle mat is made with Manila hemp. The kettle mat goes wondrously well with modern tableware.

Design: Shoko Hitomi

ITEM

**Electrical Cable Cover**
INSTRUCTIONS_P.93

Your current lighting design is nothing to complain about, but the cord is an eyesore. How about a macramé cord cover? It's simple to make.
Design: tama5

**Materials**

Hemp cord: <Large mat> 16m/18yds long /
<Small mat> 14m/16yds long

ⓐ Filler cords: <Large mat> 8m/9yds long /
<Small mat> 7m/8yds long

ⓑ Working cords: <Large mat> 8m/9yds long /
<Small mat> 7m/8yds long

Sewing thread: As needed

**Techniques**

Vertical Lark's Head Knot (see p.12)
Overhand Knot (see p.15)

1 Make a core using cord ⓐ (see "Making a Core" below).

2 Fold cord ⓑ in half and attach it to the core. Please see p.8 "Basic Mounting Knots (Reverse)". Then, tie a Vertical Lark's Head Knot to cover the core.

3 After tying knots all around the core, glue the final knot to secure.

4 Move down 5cm/2" from the final knot and tie one Overhand Knot with two strands. Trim any excess cord to complete.

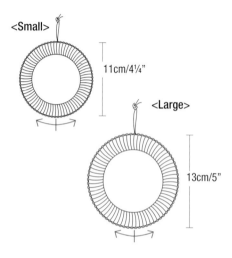

<Small> 11cm/4¼"

<Large> 13cm/5"

**Making a Core**

For a small mat, wrap cord ⓐ around a 0.5-liter plastic bottle. Use 1.5-liter plastic bottles for large mats. Bundle wrapped cord using thread at a few places.

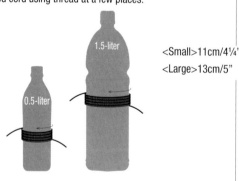

<Small>11cm/4¼"
<Large>13cm/5"

**Knotting Diagram**

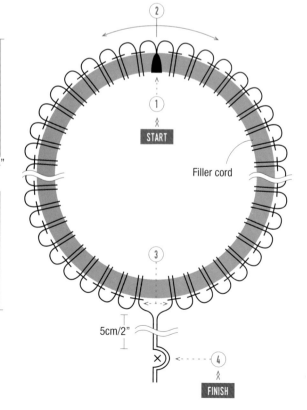

Filler cord

5cm/2"

**Materials**  Natural-color cotton cord (3mm): 13.5m/15yds long, 1 piece

**Techniques**  Spiral Knot (see p.9)

Knotting Diagram

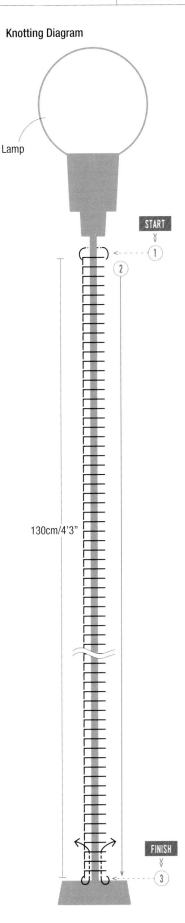

Lamp

START

130cm/4'3"

130cm/4'3"

FINISH

1 Fold the cord in half and center it on the base of the cable.

2 Use the cable as filler and tie a Spiral Knots. Tie the last three knots loosely so you can hide the end of the working cord later.

3 Weave the working end through the last three knots and pull. Tighten the last three knots using an eyelet or tweezers. Trim excess to complete.

NOTES  Adjust Length

This electrical cable cover uses the cable of a lamp you already possess and ties a Spiral Knot around the cable using cord that has been folded in half. The cable in the photo is about 130cm/4'3" long. Prepare cord that is about eleven times longer than the cable you wish to cover.

and cargoes.

# ITEM V

## Ring-Ring Hanger
### INSTRUCTIONS_P.96

# ITEM U

## Stretchy Basket

Type Ⓐ

Type Ⓑ

These baskets are made by tying "Stretch Knots." These baskets can be hung on a wall or placed on a counter. The "Ring-Ring Hanger" (top right) is quite the convenient Item. You can enjoy it as an *objet d'art*, while using it as a hanger for your jewelry and/or a belt.

Design:  Märchen Art Studio (Item U)
Etsuko Usami (Item V)

**Materials**

<Type Ⓐ>
Natural-color cotton cord (2mm):
180cm/6' x 28 pieces = 50.4m/56yds long

<Type Ⓑ>
Natural-color cotton cord (4mm):
180cm/6' x 24 pieces = 43.2m/48yd long

<Both type Ⓐ Ⓑ>
Ring: outer diameter 13cm/5", 1 piece,
transparent in color

**Techniques**  Alternating Half Hitch (see p.11)
Sailor's Knot (see p.15)

1 Fold a cord in half and mount it on the ring (see p.8 "Mounting Knot
(Double)" / Type Ⓐ: twenty-eight cords, Type Ⓑ: twenty-four cords,
mounted uniformly all around the ring).

2 Tie Stretch Knots (see below) on each cord for 13cm/5".

3 Turn your work inside-out and fold it in half. Tie a Sailor Knot using
the two facing cords to close up the bottom (Type Ⓐ: tie twenty-eight
times, Type Ⓑ: tie twenty-four times). Apply glue on each Sailor Knot
to secure. Then trim the ends short.

4 Turn your work right side out to complete.

**NOTES  About "Stretch Knot"**

A Stretch Knot is one method for making a sennit.
On each row, shift the paring of the cord by one and tie one
Alternating Half Hitch. This knot makes a basket-like diagonal
pattern and stretchy sennit.

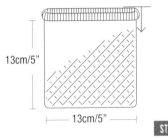

13cm/5"

├─ 13cm/5" ─┤

**Knotting Diagram**

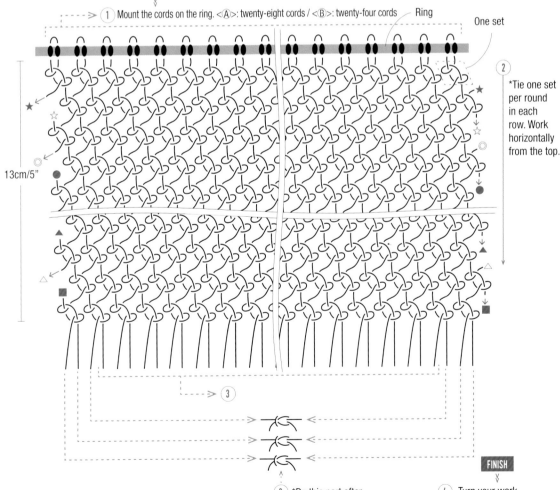

START

① Mount the cords on the ring. <Ⓐ>: twenty-eight cords / <Ⓑ>: twenty-four cords    Ring    One set

② *Tie one set
per round
in each
row. Work
horizontally
from the top.

13cm/5"

③

③ *Do this part after
turning your work
inside-out.

④ Turn your work
right side out.    95

## Materials

Natural-color cotton cord (2mm):
Approx. 26m/29yds long
ⓐ Rings on the inside loop: 8m/9yds long, 1 piece
ⓑ Rings on the outside loop: 16m/18yds long, 1 piece
ⓒ Hanging loop: 1m/4', 1 piece

Transparent plastic ring
<Large> 8cm/3" outer diameter, 3 pieces
<Small> 4cm/1½" outer diameter, 5 pieces
Natural wood piece: 1 piece

## Techniques

Alternating Half Hitch (see p.11)
Vertical Lark's Head Knot (see p.12)
Sailor's Knot (see p.15)
Gathering Knot (see p.15)
Overhand Knot (see p.15)

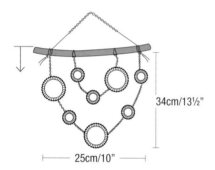

34cm/13½"

25cm/10"

1 Fold cord ⓐ in such a way that the left-side strand is 40cm/15¾" longer than the right-side. Mount cord ⓐ on the wood piece 6.5cm/2½" left of center (see p.8 "Basic Mounting Knots").

2 Tie eight Alternating Half Hitches.

3 Separate the two cords to the left and right. Use a plastic ring <small> as the base. Tie a right-facing Vertical Lark's Head Knot with the left-side cord. Also, tie a right-facing Vertical Lark's Head Knot for with the right-side cord. Tie each knot twelve times.

4 Tie Alternating Half Hitches nine times.

5 Repeat step 3 with another plastic ring <small>.

6 Tie Alternating Half Hitches eight times.

7 Separate the two cords to the left and right. Use a plastic ring <large> as the base. Tie right-facing Vertical Lark's Head Knots with the left-side cord thirty times. Tie right-facing Vertical Lark's Head Knots with the right-side cord sixteen times.

8 Tie Alternating Half Hitches eight times.

9 Refer to Knotting Diagram ❶ and warp the two cords on the wood piece 6.5cm/2½" right of center. Tie a Sailor's Knot at the back. Apply glue on the knot and trim the ends short.

10 Fold cord ⓑ in half and mount it on the wood piece 7cm/2¾" left of the cord that you mounted in step 1. Refer to Knotting Diagram ❶. Make the outside loop in a similar manner to the inner loop.

11 Refer to Knotting Diagram ❷. Make the hanging loop. Bundle two cords of ⓒ and tie one Gathering Knot about 20cm/8" in from the end of the cord.

12 Tie twenty Alternating Half Hitches.

13 Tie one Gathering Knot.

14 Move down 8cm/3" from the Gathering Knot in step 11 and tie one Overhand Knot with both cords.

15 On the left of the outer loop's mounting knot, insert the end of the wood piece between the cords and tie one Overhand Knot.

16 Move down 8cm/3" from the Gathering Knot in step 13, then repeat steps 14 through 15 to attach the other end of the hanging loop to the wood piece.

## Knotting Diagram ❷

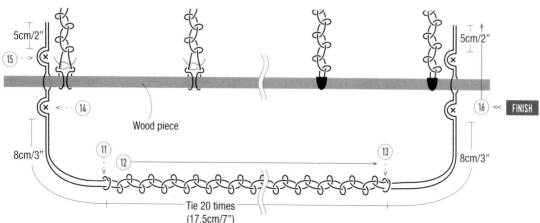

5cm/2"
15
5cm/2"
14
Wood piece
16 FINISH
8cm/3"
11
13
8cm/3"
12
Tie 20 times
(17.5cm/7")

## Knotting Diagram ❶

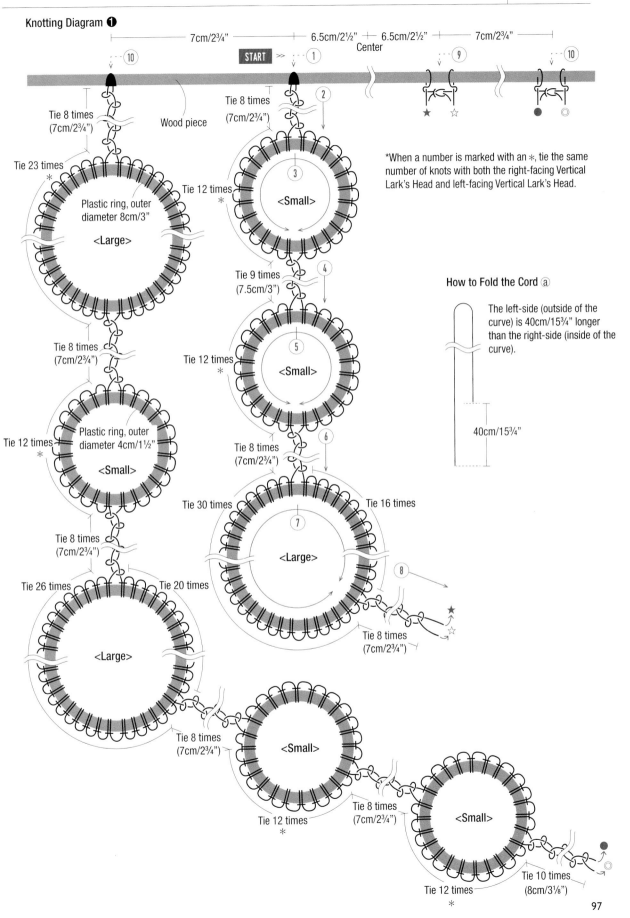

7cm/2¾"  |  6.5cm/2½"  +  6.5cm/2½"  +  7cm/2¾"
Center

⑩  START >> ①  ⑨  ⑩

Tie 8 times
(7cm/2¾")

Wood piece

Tie 8 times
(7cm/2¾")

②

Tie 23 times
*

Tie 12 times
*

③

<Small>

Plastic ring, outer
diameter 8cm/3"

<Large>

★ ☆  ● ◎

*When a number is marked with an *, tie the same
number of knots with both the right-facing Vertical
Lark's Head and left-facing Vertical Lark's Head.

Tie 9 times
(7.5cm/3")

④

Tie 8 times
(7cm/2¾")

Tie 12 times
*

⑤

<Small>

### How to Fold the Cord ⓐ

The left-side (outside of the
curve) is 40cm/15¾" longer
than the right-side (inside of the
curve).

40cm/15¾"

Tie 12 times
*

Plastic ring, outer
diameter 4cm/1½"

<Small>

Tie 8 times
(7cm/2¾")

⑥

Tie 30 times

Tie 16 times

⑦

<Large>

Tie 8 times
(7cm/2¾")

Tie 26 times

Tie 20 times

⑧

<Large>

★
☆

Tie 8 times
(7cm/2¾")

Tie 8 times
(7cm/2¾")

<Small>

Tie 8 times
(7cm/2¾")

Tie 12 times
*

<Small>

●
◎

Tie 12 times
*

Tie 10 times
(8cm/3⅛")

# ITEM W

## Floor Mat

INSTRUCTIONS_P.100

This stripe-patterned floor mat is made with sturdy jute. Jute is known as an eco-friendly material because the plant that makes jute grows quickly and its fiber is bio-degradable.

Design: Yoshimi Anai

**Materials**

White-color fine jute: 85m/93yds long / Green-color fine jute: 86m/94yds long

ⓐ Working cord: 300cm/10' long, white-color 28 pieces
ⓑ Working cord: 300cm/10' long, green-color 26 pieces
ⓒ Working cord: 400cm/13' long, green-color 2 pieces
ⓓ Filler cord: 50cm/2' long, white-color 2 pieces

**Techniques**

Square Knot (see p.10)
Alternating Square Knots (see p.10)
Vertical Lark's Head Knot (see p.12)
Reverse Clove Hitch (see p.14)
Overhand Knot (see p.15)

1 Lay out cords ⓐ through ⓒ as specified in Knotting Diagram ❶.

2 Tie knots as specified in Knotting Diagram ❶. Tie Vertical Lark's Head Knots on the leftmost and rightmost two cords on each row where green-color cords are the working cords.

3 Use a piece of cord ⓓ as the filler cord. Tie a Reverse Clove Hitch with cords ⓐ through ⓒ. Trim off the ends of the cords leaving 8cm/3" from the row of Reverse Clove Hitches.

4 Tie one Overhand Knot on both ends of cord ⓓ. Cut off excess cord and glue the knot to secure.

5 Turn your work 180 degrees (up-side down). Then tie the knots as specified in Knotting Diagram ❷. Tie Vertical Lark's Head Knots on the leftmost and rightmost two cords on each row where green-color cords are the working cords.

6 Repeat step 3.

7 Repeat step 4 to hide the ends of cord ⓓ. Complete.

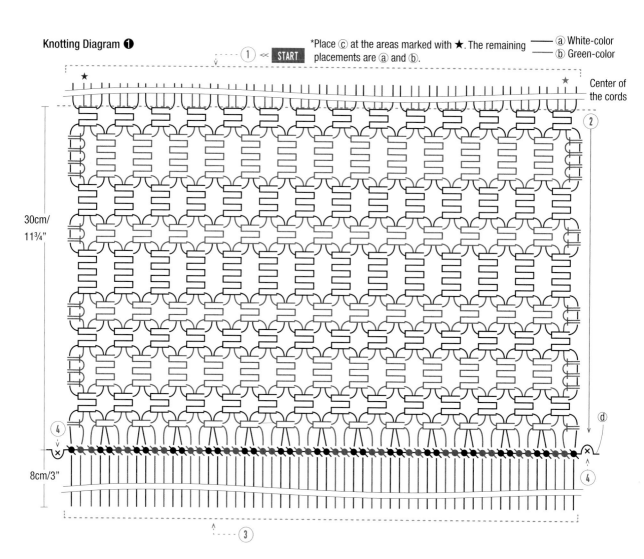

Knotting Diagram ❶

*Place ⓒ at the areas marked with ★. The remaining placements are ⓐ and ⓑ.

ⓐ White-color
ⓑ Green-color

START

Center of the cords

30cm/ 11¾"

8cm/3"

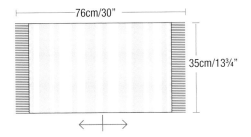

76cm/30"

35cm/13¾"

## Knotting Diagram ❷

Center of
the cords

⑤

30cm/
11¾"

⑦

8cm/3"

ⓓ

⑥

FINISH >> ⑦

Type Ⓐ

Type Ⓑ

Type Ⓐ

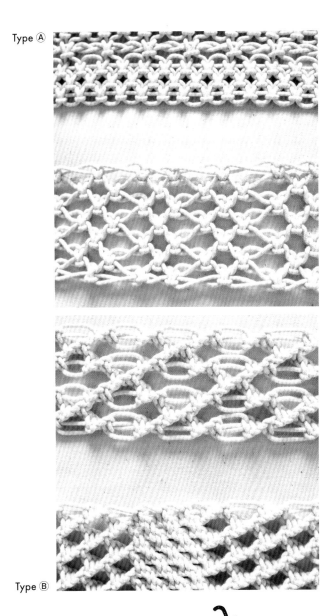

Type Ⓑ

## ITEM X

### Cushion Cover
### INSTRUCTIONS_P.104

These are original cushion covers. They are 10cm/4″ wide sennits sewn on a commercially available cushion. Each sennit is made separately so you can enjoy matching them or using different colored cords. Whatever tickles your fancy!

Design: macco (Type Ⓐ) / Chizu Tsujimoto (Type Ⓑ)

## Materials

Natural-color cotton cord (3mm)
<Type-Ⓐ> sennit: 69.7m/77yds long (3 pieces total)
<Type-Ⓑ> sennit: 82.5m/91yds long (3 pieces total)
*See "Cord Length" to cut cords
Thread: As much as necessary

## Techniques

Spiral Knot (see p.9)
Alternating Square Knots (see p.10)
Square Knot (see p.10)
3-Ply Braids (see p.13)
Horizontal Clove Hitch (see p.8)

## Cord Length

| Type | Use | | Length | Pieces |
|---|---|---|---|---|
| Ⓐ | Sennit A Working cords | ⓐ | 70cm/2'4" | 14 pcs |
| | | ⓑ | 160cm/5'3" | 20 pcs |
| | | ⓒ | 210cm/7' | 4 pcs |
| | Sennit B Working cords | ⓓ | 90cm/3' | 10 pcs |
| | | ⓔ | 160cm/5' 3" | 6 pcs |
| | Filler cords | ⓕ | 15cm/6" | 6 pcs |
| Ⓑ | Sennit C Working cords | ⓖ | 120cm/4' | 8 pcs |
| | | ⓗ | 155cm/5'1" | 20 pcs |
| | | ⓘ | 165cm/5'6" | 12 pcs |
| | Sennit D Working cords | ⓙ | 70cm/2'4" | 4 pcs |
| | | ⓚ | 160cm/5'3" | 10 pcs |
| | | ⓛ | 120cm/4' | 2 pcs |
| | Filler cords | ⓜ | 15cm/6" | 6 pcs |

Type Ⓐ requires: two pieces of Sennit A, one piece of Sennit B. Type Ⓑ requires: two pieces of Sennit C, one piece of Sennit D. Sew the required sennit on a cushion (40cm x 40cm/15¾" x 15¾"). Feel free to change the "matching" of these sennits and position their sewn sections as desired.

*The right uses steps 1 through 8 as instructions for making Type Ⓐ. Type Ⓑ uses similar steps to Type Ⓐ. When you make Type Ⓐ, use the number or letter inside these [ ] brackets and when you make Type Ⓑ, use the number or letter inside these < > brackets.

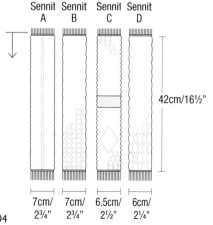

Sennit A   Sennit B   Sennit C   Sennit D

42cm/16½"

7cm/ 2¾"   7cm/ 2¾"   6.5cm/ 2½"   6cm/ 2¼"

## Knotting Diagram: Sennit A (make two sennits)

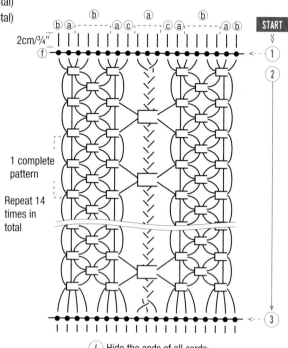

2cm/¾"

1 complete pattern

Repeat 14 times in total

START

① ② ③

④ Hide the ends of all cords.

⑤ Repeat the above to make another sennit.

★First, tie rows of 3-Ply Braids at the center. Then, move on to Alternating Square Knots.

**1** Refer to the Knotting Diagram of the sennit you are going to make. Mount the working cords on a holding cord. Holding cord: [ⓕ]<ⓜ >, Working cords: [ⓐ-ⓒ: nineteen cords] / <ⓖ-ⓘ: twenty cords> (see p.8 "Using Horizontal Clove Hitch")

**2** Tie the knots to make [Sennit A] and <Sennit C> as specified in the Knotting Diagram.

**3** Add one piece of [ⓕ]/<ⓜ >and tie a row of Horizontal Clove Hitches.

**4** Hide the ends of the cords. Weave the end of the cord into a knot at the backside and cut off excess cord. (If you wish, you can trim the ends of [ⓐ-ⓒ]-<ⓖ-ⓘ> to make a fringe.)

**5** Repeat steps 1 through 4 to make another sennit [A] or <C>.

**6** Refer to the Knotting Diagram of the sennit you are going to make. Mount the working cords on a holding cord. Holding Cord: [ⓕ]<ⓜ >, Working cords: [ⓓ and ⓔ: sixteen cords]/<ⓙ-ⓛ: sixteen cords> (see p.8 "Using Horizontal Clove Hitch")

**7** Repeat steps 2 through 4 to make one piece of sennit [B] or <D>.

**8** Sew [Sennit A·B·A] or <Sennit C·D·C> on a cushion as desired.

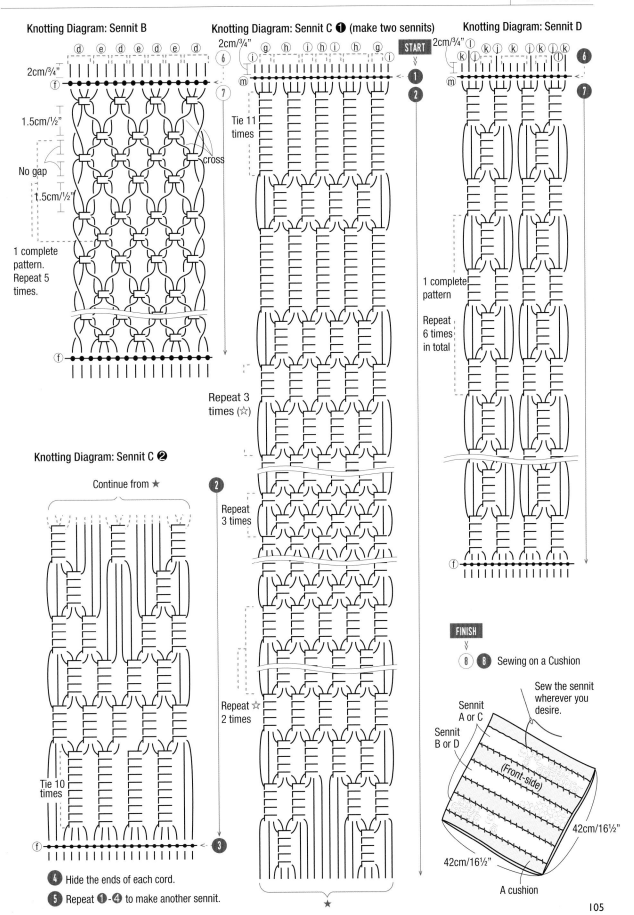

# ITEM V

## Lampshade
### INSTRUCTIONS_P.108

The design of this macramé lampshade is unique and the way the light comes through the lampshade is very attractive.

Design: Sawa Matsuda

**Materials**

Natural-color cotton cord (2mm):
150cm/5' x 88 pieces = 132m/145yds long
Metal ring: 23cm/9" diameter, 2 pieces
Hook with chain: 1 piece

**Techniques**

Square Knot (see p.10)
Alternating Square Knots (see p.10)
Horizontal Clove Hitch (see p.8)

1 Mount all cords, folded in half, on a metal ring (see p.8 "Mounting Knot (Double)").

2 Refer to the Knotting Diagram while tying knots to make a triangular shape. Tie Alternating Square Knots where each knot is two Square Knots that make a triangular shape. Work the cords to complete one complete pattern. After finishing one pattern, move on to the second. Work the cords until you finish to make the third complete pattern.

3 Tie Horizontal Clove Hitches with each cord to attach another piece of metal ring.

4 Trim the ends of the cord to 5cm/2" long. Complete.

**Knotting Diagram**

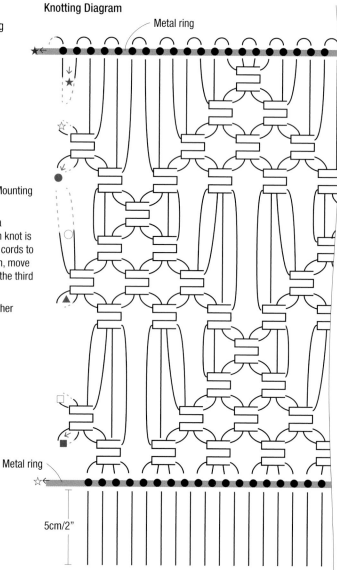

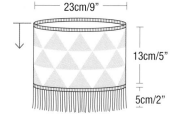

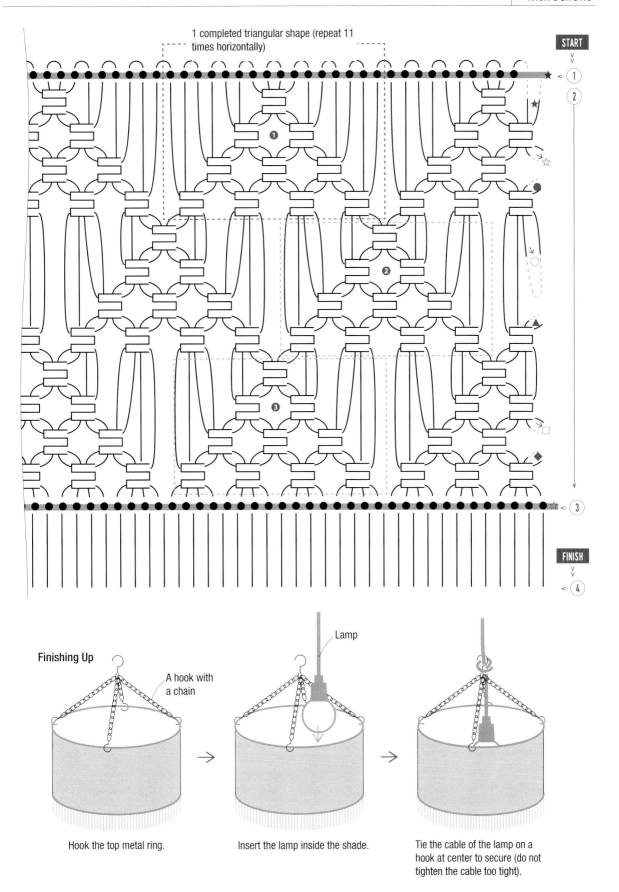

1 completed triangular shape (repeat 11 times horizontally)

START

FINISH

**Finishing Up**

A hook with a chain

Hook the top metal ring.

Lamp

Insert the lamp inside the shade.

Tie the cable of the lamp on a hook at center to secure (do not tighten the cable too tight).

# Tips for Creating Boho Style

After taking up macramé to make original interior décor items, you may start to think about changing your interior décor style to "boho style." What sort of things are "boho style" anyway? I will share with you points for creating boho style interior décor.

## POINT_01 Create bohemian flare using textiles and small décor items

"Bohemian" is the origin of the term "boho." In the fashion industry "bohemian" is used to describe a style that incorporates elements of ethnic clothing and gypsy fashion. This applies to the world of interior design. Textiles and small décor items are effective when it comes to incorporating bohemian style. Incorporate ethnic elements, like Native-American textiles or Kilim (woven textiles produced by Turkish nomads), for area rugs, lap blankets, cushion covers, or tapestries. Or, simply display small, colorful, ethnic articles. Since many of those small ethnic articles are handmade, they will bring warmth to spaces that are dominated by modern interior décor, which tends to have a sterile atmosphere.

A colorful Native-American textile rug accentuate the space. It matches perfectly with macramé items.

## POINT_02 Display plants to "invite" nature into a space

The word, bohemian, is used to describe the customs of hippies who practice unconventional lifestyles and aspire to live harmoniously with Nature. Therefore, "Nature" is an important keyword for the boho style. Houseplants are essential to incorporating elements of "Nature" into interior decoration. A large potted houseplant on the floor, cacti and succulents in small pots along the windowsill, a hanging display of cut flowers, a suspended pot of drooping vines from the ceiling—you may feel this is too much, but it actually increases the boho style feel.

The image here is about taking Nature into the room. The pot suspended from the ceiling, the hanging display of cut flowers on the wall, and the vase on the chest.

## POINT_03    Macramé items set the tone

Plant hangers, tapestries, screens—macramé items will set the tone. The macramé items introduced throughout this book are boho style essentials that dictate the tone of your décor. We encourage you to incorporate them into your overall style.

By the way, do you know why macramé work is tied to the bohemian style? The macramé craze started on the west coast of the U.S. in the 1960's and it was hippies (bohemians) who really created the fad. Hippies took notice of the fact that macramé can be used to create anything, from jewelry to interior décor items, as long as you have yarn. Also, macramé is a handcraft that has the allure of art. So, hippies enthusiastically produced macramé items. I think that what expanded the fad most back then was maybe people's aspirations toward the unconventional, natural, and artistic lifestyle of hippies. Perhaps, the reason why we feel a certain amount of comfort from having macramé items around is rooted in such aspirations.

The sample tapestry allows you to enjoy different knots all at once—it is an excellent example for understanding the depth of macramé art.

## POINT_04    Mix and match to create a relaxing space

So far, I have discussed how to incorporate bohemian-style items into your décor. The next thing is mixing bohemian-style items with other styles as desired. Actually, this is the core of boho style. Rooms that have uniform décor look quite fashionable. However, that décor often lacks that inviting and relaxing feel. But, mixing and matching other styles of décor will create a relaxing and comfortable room. This is the reason why the boho style is so popular.

For example, combining traditional textiles and a modern sofa, or displaying graphic art beside a macramé tapestry, putting plants in a Scandinavian-style ceramic as a hanging display, etc...

"As you desire" is the key phrase here. Mix and match your favorite items to create truly comfortable spaces—this is the most important thing when creating boho style interior décor.

The retro-pop plaid patterned floor and macramé screen, vintage modern chair, poster art—blending all of these different elements creates a relaxed and comfortable space.

Author Profile

## Märchen Art Studio

Märchen Art Studio is a creators' group organized by MÄRCHEN ART Inc. in Japan. MÄRCHEN ART Inc. is a company that designs and sells leather, hemp cord, jewelry parts, and other craft items. Märchen Art Studio holds workshops at the group's studio in Ryogoku, Tokyo. Also, the group publishes works in books to introduce fashionable crafts that effectively use materials and suggest new ways of enjoying macramé work.

## Macramé Décor
25 Boho-Chic Patterns and Project Ideas

by Märchen Art Studio

Copyright © 2017 Graphic-sha Publishing Co., Ltd.
Text copyright © 2017 Graphic-sha Publishing Co., Ltd.
Macramé designs copyright © 2017 MÄRCHEN ART Inc.

First published in Japan in 2017 by :
Graphic-sha Publishing Co., Ltd.

English edition published in 2018 by:
NIPPAN IPS Co., Ltd.
1-3-4, Yushima
Bunkyo-ku, Tokyo, 113-0034

ISBN 978-4-86505-168-1

Printed in China

### Creative staff

| | |
|---|---|
| Artwork design: | Yoshimi Anai, anudo, Yoshie Ichikawa, Etsuko Usami, Miyuki Ozaki, tama5, Yuko Tsukahara, Chizu Tsujimoto, Michiko Nakamura, Aki Hagino, Shoko Hitomi, macco, Sawa Matsuda, Märchen Art Studio |
| Technical supervisor: | The Japan Macramé Association |
| Photo styling: | Kanae Ishii |
| Photography: | Satoshi Nagare, Ryohei Sasatani (pp. 3-7, 16-17, 22-23, 46-47, 66-67) |
| Video production: | Ryohei Sasatani |
| Illustration: | Yuriho Koike |
| Project planning: | Yoshiko Kasai (Graphic-sha Publishing Co., Ltd.) |

### English edition

| | |
|---|---|
| English translation: | Kevin Wilson |
| Layout: | Shinichi Ishioka |
| Production and management: | Kumiko Sakamoto (Graphic-sha Publishing Co., Ltd.) |